MORE MORELLO LETTERS

Pen pal to the super stars

by

Duncan McNair

MONSTER PUBLICATIONS • London

In memory of Stella and David
and their numerous kindnesses

Published in Great Britain in 2011 by
Monster Publications
53a Park View Road
Ealing
London W5 2JF

Copyright © Duncan McNair 2011

Cover illustrations copyright © Steve Crisp
Text illustrations copyright © Nicola Bradley
Book design by Mousemat Design Limited

The right of Duncan McNair to be identified as the author of this work has been asserted
by him in accordance with the Copyright, Designs and Patents Act 1988

A catalogue for this item is available from the British Library

ISBN: 978 0 9563422 2 5

Printed in the UK by CPI William Clowes Beccles NR34 7TL

Explanatory notes on the text:

1. the letters sent by the Morellos contain content which is fictional and which is not intended to be taken as a factual account or representation of any matters related therein.

2. the use herein of Molerro, Molierro and other variations on Morello is a low-tech response to the power and reach of the ubiquitous search engine. The device is employed to preserve Mrs Morello's modesty from detection until she judges the moment has arrived to reveal herself to her correspondent.

3. the sketches festooning the letters were applied after the correspondence had closed.

4. the "BK" device at the head of page 39 is a substitute for the device normally used by the Burger King company which is protected by law.

MORE MORELLO LETTERS

Pen pal to the super stars

Acknowledgments

The tentative start to this project, many years ago now, has given way to prodigious exchanges of correspondence. Mrs Morello is still posted at her escritoire, pounding out missives to the great and the good, surrounded by the ever-helpful denizens of her menageries, and the negligibly helpful Mr Morello and the kids.

It is five years since the publication of *The Morello Letters*, the predecessor volume to this book. When to my stupefaction the book soared up the rankings to Number 1 in Amazon and elsewhere for humour-parody, Mrs Morello lay down the goat feed, sharpened her pen and hammered the keys even harder.

The Morellos' capacity for misapprehension as to everything has bloomed, and the desire of the superstars to provide clarification remains undimmed. Almost without exception this has been done with grace and the greatest good humour. And when (with the author's assistance) the Morellos have blown their cover to their interlocutors, initial discombobulation has given way to high amusement and laughter.

So I thank heartily all those who have embraced the Morellos' epistolary musings: statesmen, CEOs, archbishops, distinguished academics and University Chancellors, heads of City law firms, ombudsmen, Olympic organisers, curators of national art galleries and museums, journalists and TV stars, hotel proprietors, and the great fraternity of British goat lovers. And (of course) nudists. They are, after all, co-authors of the book.

Next, I wish to acknowledge my debt to everyone who has helped this book towards its production. I renew my thanks to all those mentioned in the predecessor volume. But more have since joined the caravan. Amongst my fellow travellers who have supported the project in many ways are Sheila Pardese, Bernard Stirzaker and family, Tara Wessely, Montse Garcia, Ian Cooper, Ricardo and Alexandra Cardenas, Mark House, Julie Order, Diarmuid Flood, Nicholas Bacon QC, Lord McNair, Professor Malcolm Troup and the brilliantly talented and modest Nicola Bradley. Also for the pure technical production Steve Crisp, Ian Hughes and Andy Howarth – a formidable trinity.

I must also recognise the extravagant kindness shown by the Morellos' many reviewers whose collective support has borne the heroes of this book far beyond what was ever imagined. I wish I could thank them each in person. They have proved indubitably that goats have legs.

Finally I am sincerely grateful to all those who have generously given permission to reproduce their correspondence in these pages.

Duncan McNair
Morello Mansions
Ealing

July 2011

Park View Road
Ealing
London W5

29 September 2004

The Most Reverend and Honourable Rowan Williams BA DPhil DD FBA
The Archbishop of Canterbury
Lambeth Palace
London SE1 7JU

Dear Reverend Archbishop

I write respectfully and with some trepidation to make a small request.

Mrs Morello and I have three children, the youngest being Rizzo (7). He's been a thorn in our side for some time, coming last in most subjects at school and no good at all at sports. However the one thing that has caught his interest is animals – from every corner of that kingdom in fact. In the hope of settling him down, Mrs Morello (Rosetta) has bought him various little pets. But he's got into the annoying habit of claiming people he sees bear a resemblance to them. Now his class teacher Ms Fosdyke has set a project whereby each child has to produce a photo of a family or neighbour's pet, and also of a famous person the creature resembles.

At long last Rizzo feels on a level playing field with his classmates. His little gerbil Dandy (sold to us incidentally as Derek but urgently renamed) has produced a litter of 8 babies, now 2 weeks old with eyes open, and bits of fur. Rizzo saw you on television and immediately yelled out "*gebrils*" (he can't get the name quite right).

Would you consent to Rizzo naming one of the little mites in your honour, we thought Wee Billy, or Cantab possibly? This is a little unusual but here's hoping you'll feel able to agree given the exceptional-circumstances-on-this-occasion. We could always send you a snap of the rodent-in-question.

If you can't help we can always apply elsewhere. Mrs Morello feels quite strongly that one of the other babies looks quite like Sir Cliff Richard.

Thank you so much for your attention to this small matter,

Yours sincerely

RM Morello (Mr)

LAMBETH PALACE

Revd Jonathan Jennings
Archbishop's Press Secretary

Mr R M Morello
Park View
Ealing
London W5

20th October 2004

Dear Mr Morello,

Thank you for writing to the Archbishop on the question of names of your son's gerbils.

A nice try.

No, really.

Yours sincerely,

Revd Jonathan Jennings
Archbishop's Press Secretary

Lambeth Palace, London SE1 7JU
Switchboard: +44(0)20 7898 1200   Fax: +44(0)20 7261 9836
Email: jonathan.jennings@lampal.c-of-e.org.uk

Park View Road
Ealing
London W5

16 November 2004

The Reverend Jonathan Jennings
Press Secretary to the Archbishop of Canterbury
Lambeth Palace
London SE1 7JU

Dear Reverend Jennings

Thank you very much from the whole Morello family for taking the time to reply to my letter of 29 September and on the matter of the Archbishop and gerbils.

Your letter was quite short and we thought perhaps a bit was left out. I find short letters difficult to write as there seem to be so many words to fit in. Especially in Italian. We've never had such a tiddler before! (though the gas board wrote us a short letter in 1986 which we didn't like as we'd made a mistake about a bill and they were quite angry. We didn't like that letter. Unlike yours).

Mrs Morello has told me to apologise for writing to the Archbishop in the first place. She asks me to point out that His Eminence does not resemble a gerbil. Anyway there are no names left for the baby gerbs - they've all been matched up with famous celebrities etc!

I apologise for any inconvenience which may have been caused and am very sorry to disappoint His Eminence on this occasion.

Thanking you,

Yours sincerely

RM Morello

PS: Is there any chance H.E. would consent to a guinea pig match possibly? We could do a really good one with strong bristles and sharp teeth etc. Hoping this is acceptable. Please reply to me not the Mrs.

PPS: could I ask for a photo of HE the Archbishop for our second, Amphora (14), who was too shy to ask but said he is "cute".

A Nicer try!

As requested,

[signature] Jonathan Jennings

⊕ THE CHURCH
OF ENGLAND

LAMBETH PALACE

Lambeth Palace Press Office

Lambeth Palace
London SE1 7JU

Telephone: +44(0)20-7898 1280
Fax: +44(0)20-7261 1761
Website: www.archbishopofcanterbury.org

Photo: Eleanor Bentall

END OF CORRESPONDENCE

Park View Road
Ealing
London W5
1 October 2004

Lord Coe
Chairman - London 2012
50th Floor, 1 Canada Square
London E14 5LT

Dear Lord Coe

I am writing to offer the support of the Morello family in your leadership of the bid to bring the Olympic Games to our capital City in 2012. In fact we only moved to London some years ago, from a small but charming dairy farm in Devon. I still feel great loyalty to that county, though the concept of a campaign to bring the Olympics to Paignton is one the IOC is maybe not ready for. Perhaps in 2016, in the unlikely event the London bid unravels?

Could I possibly observe that anything which spreads the Olympic ideal to a global audience in a way which recognises no cultural barriers and draws us together as a family of nations can only be good? With this in mind can I respectfully suggest some new events for inclusion in the London bid:

1 snake charming;

2 throwing the Wellington boot (this is an old village tradition in Somerset);

3 Morris dancing (less common now but once popular amongst village folk of limited intelligence);

4 chasing lions (the idea is that competitors tweak the tail and then run away. This reverses the Christians and lions theme but no one gets eaten – hopefully!);

5 measuring crocodiles (again, not for the faint hearted). The better version is to have to arrange three crocodiles in a line nose to tail and then measure. Great fun!

6 hanging upside down like a bat (painful and very difficult). I believe Japanese audiences will enjoy this hugely.

These are only a few ideas. I have some more too if you like them. We all feel that they could give London the edge. We hope London wins as Mrs Morello has bad feet and the thought of a trip overseas worries her.

I shall politely await your comments. If you don't deal directly with the details could you perhaps pass this on to the nuts and bolts man (or woman) possibly?

Sincerely yours
RM Morello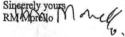

PS: are you still running, or perhaps doing judo in the games with Rt Hon William Hague? (Mrs Morello says you must be fit to get up to your office if the lift breaks).

PPS: our second, Amphora (14), asks for your autograph if possible, perhaps. She is too shy to write for herself.

CANDIDATE CITY

RM Morello
Park View Road
Ealing
London W5
16 December 2004

Seb Coe has asked me to contact you to thank for your recent letters and support for the Bid.

Thank you for your interesting ideas for new events to be included, if London were to get the Olympic Games in 2012. You may be interested to know that in order for a sport to be included in the Olympic Games, there are certain requirements that have to be fulfilled. This includes being widely practiced by men in at least 75 countries and on three continents, and by women in at least 40 countries and on three continents.

We have now entered a new and crucial phase of our campaign where we are able to promote London 2012 internationally as well as domestically. Your support is vital to us as we strive to maximise support from all over the United Kingdom.

Thank you so much for writing.

With best wishes,

Nicola Milan
Office of Sebastian Coe OBE

London 2012 Ltd 1 Canada Square Canary Wharf London E14 5LT
Telephone +44 (0)20 7093 5000 Fax +44 (0)20 7093 5001 www.london2012.org

Registered in London. Company number 4829558

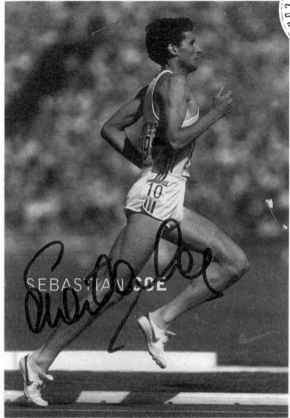

SEBASTIAN COE

SEBASTIAN **COE**

NAME : SEBASTIAN COE

PERSONAL BESTS : 800m 1.41.73 mins
1500m 3.29.77 mins / MILE 3.47.33 mins

WORLD RECORDS : 800m 1.41.73 mins (1981)
1000m 2.12.18 mins (1981) / 1500m 3.32.03 mins (1979)
MILE 3.47.33 mins (1981)

OLYMPIC GAMES :
MOSCOW 1980 - 1500m GOLD / 800m SILVER
LOS ANGELES 1984 - 1500m GOLD / 800m SILVER

FOR MORE INFORMATION ON NIKE : www.nike.com

FOR MORE INFORMATION ON
NIKE RUNNING EMAIL : uk.runners@nike.com

Park View Road
Ealing
London W5

25 November 2004

The Head of Research
Kellogg College
Wellington Square
OXFORD OX1 2JA

Dear Sir

I and the Mrs have always enjoyed your products. However we have a tiny bone to pick ref the cornflakes.

You always used to have little plastic battleships in the packets. And dinosaurs. Our youngest (Rizzo) has been trying to collect more of the prehistoric reptiles which he inherited from Tosti, his older brother. But now they've stopped appearing with the flaky corns and he can't seem to find a:

        - stegosaurus, or a

        - brachiosaurus, or a

        - brontosaurus.

However the lad has 2 (two) Tyrannosaurus (Rexes). So could he send you back one Tyranno in exchange for a steg or a brach? (or a bront?).

Also, do you have a spare Type 40 destroyer (with 2 gun turrets)?

Hoping for some good news soon.

Best wishes

RM Morello

RM Morello

PS: I have quite a good idea for a new breakfast cereal. It came to me when the mrs shoved off for the weekend leaving the pantry as good as bare. It's to do with the bedding on the rabbits' cage. Shred it then add milk (and sugar to taste). It's if there's nothing else in the house.

PPS: We could go halves if it catches on. Keep mum for the moment.

PPPS: Mrs Schneider feels the pterodactyl looks rather like Rizzo's pet parrot (Russell). She says it's to do with the beak.

Park View Road
Ealing
London W5

19 October 2004

President George W Bush
The White House
1600 Pennsylvania Avenue NW
Washington DC 20500
USA
By fax

Dear President Bush

I am writing from Ealing (Europe) to wish you and Senator Dick Cheney (the Vice President) and the whole election team all the best for the Presidential Election on November 2nd!!

We thought you socked it to 'em in the Presidential Debates. Tall urbane smooth and articulate. Mrs Morello (Rosetta) who is in pain constantly from ingrowing toenails stopped moaning for the first time in weeks when you came on the screen, then her breathing rate picked up noticeably. We didn't understand much of what you were saying as it was full of sums etc, but there again nor did Senator Kerry!

Have you been in the movies, or was that Roland Reagan ? (a former president).

Does it help to be really tall to become President? Tosti (17) our eldest is studying sociology and modern politics (or something) , and is aiming for a place at university to do *Politico-Sociological trends in modern autonomous nation states*. At East Rutlandshire University. In 2007. (he needs 2 C's and an F).

Tosti has read somewhere that each of the last 26 Presidents of the USA has been taller than the previous one. As Pres Clinton was c 6'2", we measured on the screen at home that you are about 6 foot 7 inches. In your socks. Or maybe 7 foot. Is this true please sir?

As we have had a few problems in our family but love the US we would be honoured if you or (if you're busy at present) maybe one of your family or a "co-worker" could send us a message or note or something. We're working hard here for your election!

Best wishes and God's blessings

Yours most respectabfully

RM Morello

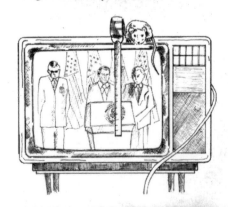

Mr Morrello,

God Bless

Sincerely

[signature: George W. Bush]

Park View Road
Ealing
London W5

2 January 2005

The Secretary
Ribble Valley Club
Near Blackburn
Lancashire

Dear Sir or Madam

I hope you may be able to assist in a certain matter.

I think you are a club where people take off their clothes in front of each other, even their socks and underwear. Then walk around in the altogether, and play ping pong.

We Morellos believe disrobing in public is wicked, and naughty. It might also encourage other unusual things to happen, considering what you might see.

Can I come along to the club one Sunday with a Bible and preach to your members (so to speak)? I'll be wearing lots of clothes, and I can look the other way so I don't see too much.

The wife reckons she'll accompany me. She says she'll wear a blindfold, though she's a bit large and your members might need blindfolds as well in case she arrives starkers.

Hoping to hear soon, thanking you

RM Morello

Ribble Valley Club
Lancashire

Mr R M Morello
Park View Road
Ealing
London
W5

Dear Mr Morello

Thank you for your letter, and we apologise for our lateness in replying. Your letter, as with others of its type, was brought to our Committee meeting, where it gave us much enjoyment.

We are indeed, as you say, "a club where people take off their clothes in front of each other" – though to be strictly accurate we tend to take our clothes off behind or to the side of each other, as the act is not performed as a form of ritual display, as you may be implying. The removal of socks is not considered to be compulsory, though some of us hold the opinion that they look really silly with sandals, and others find they tend to get rather muddy in inclement weather.

It is a great pity that the Morellos believe that disrobing in public is "wicked and naughty". We feel that life is just a bowl of cherries, and the ripe ones look best on display. This does not lead to any unusual activities – unless you consider volleyball particularly unusual, and it has to be said that rushing about playing it on a hot Sunday afternoon when you could just be lazing in the sun is considered to be unusual by some of our members.

You would be welcome at our Club any Sunday should you choose to visit (making arrangements beforehand of course, as is routine). If you wait until the weather is better, you may even find that you do not need to wear lots of clothes, and might even dare to bare with us. Regarding your wife – really, a blindfold isn't necessary. There's nothing here she won't have seen before, unless you have a more-than-unusually-staid married life. In fact as she is, by your own comment, a larger lady, we would positively welcome her – there is no sizeism in naturism; she will probably feel very comfortable here (especially if she has to put up with comments about her figure such as those expressed in your letter).

Yours, in naturism,

Di Timmin

For the members of the Ribble Valley Club.

Park Veiw Road
Ealing
London W5

8 September 2005

Head of Customer Services
Sainsbury's Super Markets
33 Hoblorn
London EC1N 2HT

Dear Mr Sainsbury's Man/Lady

At school Miss Tibbings told us that a lady bought a load of bananas at the Co-op and took them home. Then some spidery thing ran out and bit her hand and she fell over and her arm nearly fell off.

Well I was at Sainsbury's with my mum and dad and Tank (our bulldog pup) last Saturday morning after swimming. When we got home I was helping my mum by unpacking the shopping in the kitchen.

Suddenly I spotted a scorpion which ran out of a cauliflour. Then it kept hanging around. I thought it was quite nice as it seemed to be smiling. Then it was waving few of its legs around like it was saying "cheerio, catch you later". Then it ran away (sideways). I think it hid behind a potato.

A bit later Mum was in the lounge and sat down. Then she screamed and said she felt something very sharp stick in her. She said it felt just like a scorpion would if you sat on one. She leapt up and dropped a spode china pot which smashed everywhere. Mum says she never gets her facts wrong and that she saw a pot just like that one on Antiques Showboat on BBC telly which was worth about a million quid.

As the spider lady got a few quid could we have even more?

Yours sincerely

Rizzo Morello

Rizzo Morello (aged 7)

PS: Mum said to write this letter. She's after a new tea cosy. And a pair of net curtains.

Sainsbury's

Our reference: 1-133366585

19 September 2005

Sainsbury's Supermarkets Ltd
33 Holborn
London
EC1N 2HT

Telephone 0800 636262
www.sainsburys.co.uk

Miss Rizzo Morello
Park View Road
Ealing
London

Dear Rizzo

Thank you for your letter. I am sorry to hear that a scorpion bit your mum on the bum after it came out of a cauliflower that she bought from the Co-op. Having been bit on the bum by a tiger that came out of some Tesco waffles, I fully appreciate how disappointing this must have been.

At Sainsbury's, we want all our customers to be happy with the products that they buy. We have lots of men in white coats who remove any scorpions from our fresh produce before it gets sent to our stores. This stops our customers having a late night run in with any bored creepy crawlies. It looks like the Co-op should also employ some of these men in white coats. That way, customers like your mum and the lady Mrs Tibbings told you about would not have had such nasty experiences.

To thank you for writing in I have enclosed a voucher. It may not cover the cost of a tea cosy or new curtains, but I hope your mum uses it to buy some cream for her bottom. Or some strong insect repellent.

Thank you once again for your letter.

Yours sincerely

Ellen Nightingale
Customer Response Team

Enclosed: £5.00 voucher

END OF CORRESPONDENCE

Registered office as above
Registered number 3261722 England
A subsidiary of J Sainsbury plc

Park View Road

Ealing

London W5

10September 2005-0

The Senior Partner
Linklaters and Alliance (solicitors)
One Silk Street
London EC2Y 7HQ

Dear Sir

I am looking for a job as a typist somewhere and thought I'd like to try you.

I've got a few dipplomas and and exccelent typing skills. I can do about 60 or 70 pwm (words per minute) depending how long are the words are. A friend of mine Trudey Smallpeice once worked for you I think.

Please can you sort me out with a good job. Then I'd like to go on to be a solicitor, and then possibly even a lawyer after that.

My hobbeys are creative things and watching TV, and wild animals. I also like pot noodles and making desserts. I help out in Dad;s bakery, in the cakes section.

Do you have a staff canteen, and please may I enquire how long are the lunch breaks?

Thank you for your interest.

Yours sincerely

Amphora. Morello (Miss)

Linklaters

One Silk Street
London EC2Y 8HQ
Telephone (44-20) 7456 2000
Facsimile (44-20) 7456 2222
Group 4 Fax (44-20) 7374 9318
DX Box Number 10 CDE

Miss Amphora Morello
Park View Road
Ealing
London
W5

22 September 2005

Dear Miss Morello

Linklaters application

Thank you for your application for a position with us.

Regrettably I have to inform you that we do not have any vacancies for someone with your particular level of experience and skills at the present time.

I am sorry that we are unable to take your application further and wish you every success in your search for a suitable position.

Thank you for your interest in Linklaters.

Yours sincerely

Chris Leigh
HR Assistant

//

Park View Road
Ealing
London W5

30 September 2005

Ms Diane Abbott MP
MP for Hacney
House of Commons
Westminster
London SW1A OAA

Dear Ms Abbott

I was shocked to hear you state very clearly on my radio last weekend that as the Member of Parliament for Hacney you *"feel there are too low levels of crime throughout my constiuenuency"*.

Whilst it is, I grant you, irresponsible to stereotype all types of criminal activity as wrong and there must be exceptions to every rule, to claim that generally crime should be driven up just to keep pace with other areas which are rushing ahead and may get grants etc is surely an assault upon our citizens' ears etc!

Surely Ladies should be a moderating influence in parliament when near the Gents?

I would be grateful if you would consider withdrawing this policy when you have a moment before harm is caused to someone unnnecessary.

Yours sincerely

RM Morello (Mr)

cc: Anne Widdicombe
    Michael Portillo

DIANE ABBOTT

Member of Parliament for Hackney North and Stoke Newington
HOUSE OF COMMONS, LONDON SW1A 0AA

24 Answering Service: (020) 7219 3000   Parliamentary Telephone: (020) 7219
E-mail address: drejerc@parliament.uk   Parliamentary Facsimile: (020) 7219

Mr R.M. Morello
Park View Road
London W5

7th November 2005

Dear Mr Morello,

Thank you for your letter regarding crime in Hackney.

Thank you for listening to me on the radio. However, you must have misheard me. I did not say that crime levels are too low in Hackney. Unfortunately they are still too high.

I am in fact working very hard to ensure that crime in Hackney, especially violent crime and gun crime, is being effectively tackled.

Please do not hesitate to contact me again in the future should you have any further queries.

Yours sincerely,

Diane Abbott MP

END OF CORRESPONDENCE

Park View Road
Ealing
London W5

13 October 2005

The Managing Director
RM Design
34 Chestnut Grove
New malden
Surrey KT3 3JN

Dear Sir

I am organising a rather large surprise event at my home. I would be most grateful if you could quote me a price for the following signs, each in nice bold characters 2" high on board or vinyl:

1   no carol singers;

2   porn stars' parking only;

3   please replace gnomes after use;

4   bishops to the left, actresses to the right;

5   please ensure curtains are completely closed before commencement;

6   pizza deliveries by side entrance only;

7   beware of the ferret.

These are a little urgent so I would be most obliged to receive your terms of business shortly. Cost should not be a problem.

Could you suggest any other suitable signs for the event to ensure it's a success?

Please reply to me, **not** the wife.

Many thanks,

Sincerely yours

RM Morello (Mr)

RM Design
34 Chestnut Grove
New Malden
Surrey
KT3 3JN

17 October 2005

Dear Mr Morello,
Thank you for your letter enquiring about signs. We can certainly help you prepare those
you specify. Our terms of business are enclosed.

Also on offer is a standard range of party signs that you can choose from, Perhaps most
suitable for you would be the Elite range (listed below) which consists of the ten most
frequently requested party signs among our regular customers.

Endoscopy unit
Stoat
Weasel
Mole
Vaseline
Trout
Vole
Halibut
Ferret
Trousers

All signs are edible of course. By the way, I see your initials are the same as mine.
Perhaps we're related.

Yours,

Roger Murphy (Managing Director, RM Design)

END OF CORRESPONDENCE

RM Design, 34 Chestnut Grove, New Malden, Surrey, KT3 3JN
Tel: 020 8949 0532 **Fax:** 020 8942 4657 **e-mail:** rogermurphy@rmdesign.co.uk

Park View Road
Ealing
London W5

13 October 2005

The Senior Lady in Waiting
The Constance Spry School of Etiquette
Moor Park House
Moor Park Lane
Farnham
Surrey GU1 8EN

Dear Ma'am

The Mrs (Rosetta) has stated after research into the leading Schools of Etiquette that above everyone you are in a position to advise on matters of do's and don't's to do with social things in polite households and parks/castles etc. These may be different to Italia, where we pinch ladies' fundaments and whistle, and blow kisses etc without reprisals, or being attacked per handbag etc.

Young Rizzo (our 3rd, age 7) came back from school on Tuesday with a question that we can't answer here, and he is kindly asking for your assistance on this:

" Which item of clothing should you remove if meeting a member of the Royal Family:

    1. your tie; or

    2. your hat; or

    3. your trousers?"

As no-one in the United Kingdom (England, Kent etc) wears hats anymore in the 20th Century it must be 1. or 3. innit? but it can't be 1. either since I believe a gentleman always sports a tie in proper circles, but it can't be the troos could it? We just wondered.

Sorry my Inglis is up to no good.

Thanking you. You would be much appreciated.

Yours sincerely

RM Morello (Mr)

Park View Road
Ealing
London W5

25 October 2005

Mrs Martine Frost
Director of Courses for Etiquette and Good Living
The Constance Spry School of Etiquette
Moor Park House
Moor Park Lane
Farnham
Surrey GU1 8EN

Dear Ma'am

I am writing ref.my letter of 13 October of which I attach a further copy hereto.

I am very sorry not to have heard from the Constance Spry School. The wife (Rosetta) feels it is because as an Italian my Englis languages is very poor and I have not been properly understood about the matter raised for our small son Rizzo.

We have heard a lot of recommendations regarding your School and hope you could reply?

Do you also have a brochure you could provide as Mrs M feels our second, Amphora, needs a little bit of polishing by your staff as she is hopeless in polite companies. She slouches badly and has no interest in arranging flowers or dancing which must be every father's wish for their only daughter considering she is of limited intelllect and made a mess of her examinations.

Anyway the wife's decided we don't want her going to "Uni" where she'll fall in with the wrong sort and be into drugs and worse in the wife's opinion and she could do with some country air.

I should be most grateful for your terms of business.

Thanking you,

Yours sincerely

RM Morello (Mr)

MOOR PARK HOUSE, MOOR PARK LANE
FARNHAM, SURREY GU10 1QP

9 REASONS WHY YOU SHOULD CHOOSE CONSTANCE SPRY

- **TRADITION** Constance Spry revolutionised Flower Design and founded the now world famous company in 1928
- **LOCATION** We are centrally located close to airports, railway station and leading tourist attractions
- **COURSES** We offer the best training available today in Flower Design providing the widest range of course and highest level of skill
- **SIZE** Small groups ensure that maximum individual attention is always available as personal advice on a range of extra curricular matters
- **RESULTS** Many of our students go on to set up their own business or work for prestigious names in the industry in the UK or Abroad
- **STYLE** Traditional but timeless our style is adaptable and always suitable
- **TEAM** Our tutors, demonstrators and decorators are highly skilled and experienced. They are always available to help you make a choice or plan an event
- **REFERENCES** Word of mouth accounts for a high proportion of our business.
- **TRACK RECORD** Our design skills are in demand from such prestigious organisations as Government Hospitality and London Livery Companies

Park View Road
Ealing
London W5

5 December 2005

Mrs Martine Frost
Director of Courses for Etiquette and Good Living
The Constance Spry School of Etiquette
Moor Park House
Moor Park Lane
Farnham
Surrey GU1 8EN

Dear Ma'am

Thank you so much for sending the brochure over regarding the Constance Spry School. We discussed it at length on the kitchen table last Saturday evening.

After a long and democratic discussion involving the whole family, Mrs Morello has decided that Amphora will be enrolled at your School.

Should we send the sub. now for the first term? Is it on a season ticket basis? Also, can we be sure of the following treatments for the girl:

> Poise;
> Posture
> Elocutions
> Flower arrangements

We noticed in your pics a young lass walking slowly down the stairs with several books on her head, which seemed a good idea.

Would Amphora be able to meet some suitable young gents for social exchanges , and political thoughts etc - under the supervision of a lady-in-waiting?

Could we bring her down say on 18 December to get matters underway without delay? Can she bring a couple of pets, one in a jam jar?

Many thanks and look forward to hearing. We have heard excellent reports of your academy.

Yours sincerely

RM Morello (Mr)

Park View Road
Ealing
London W5

26 November 2005

The Leader of the Council
Beccles Town Council
The Walk
Beccles NR34 9AJ

Dear Sir or Madam

Ref: The Olympic Games

I have recently been assisting Lord Coe on consultatitive aspects etc of the bid for the Olympics, which has been successful (for London). I am now wishing to build on this success with reference to future Games.

After extensive research across the most promising parts of the UK, and bits of Wales, Mrs Morello and I are able to announce that the ideal venue for the Meeting of the Thirty First Olympiad in 2016 is …**Beccles.** We know the area, having once got lost, and went back there last year as we'd made friends with the couple who live quite near the Stairlift Centre, though unfortunately they were out at the time. We absolutely love the area and its peoples.

Would you be interested in your name going forward for this prestigious event? We think Beccles has a much stronger potential than any of the others – Los Angeles, Tokyo, Mexico City, and Bingley. Some of the key elements are already in place. Enquiries reveal you already have a Macdonald's, and a slide, and that there's a telephone kiosk down by the skateboarding centre.

Do you have an MP for your area? Don't worry if you're not allowed one due size etc, but if you have and he/she's done a bit of running this could be an advantage. There will be some forms to fill in but this shouldn't take long. Anyway you can always do them at home or online at the library (on a computer).

Hoping to hear soon. I apologise for the poor English due to being Italain.

Best of luck and good wishes etc

Yours sincerely

RM Morello (Mr)

BECCLES TOWN COUNCIL

Town Hall,
The Walk,
Beccles,
Suffolk,
NR34 9AJ

Mr R M Morello
Park View Road
Ealing
LONDON   W5

9 December 2005

Dear Mr Morello

Thank you for your correspondence dated 26th November 2005, the contents have been noted.

I have spoken to our Mayor, Councillor Sigsworth, but regret to inform you that Beccles would be far too small for such a prestigious event and therefore will have to decline your offer.

Kind regards.

Yours sincerely

Jula Aldred
Acting Town Clerk

Park View Road
Ealing
London W5

28 November 2005

Lord McNair
House of Lords
Westminster
London SW1A OAA

Dear M'Lud

I write to you as a senior member of the House of Lords to request your advisories on a constitutional problem.

The wife (Rosetta) reckons the country need more ladies upstairs than we've already got. She seems to have undertaken an extensive academic survey as to which figures from modern Brit. Society should be lined up for this honour. This has involved colossal visits to her friends at Irene's hair salon down East Acton, and at the Ladies' Stoats Club which meets at the Empire most Tuesday evenings.

As a result the wife is able to announce that after an exhaustive enquiry involving the expression of numerous expert opinions by leading political commentators across the spectrum a single strong candidate has emerged to become a lady lord. Herself.

I'm in favour of this as it'll get her out and about away from Ealing. She's also good at leaping up and yelling while waving the newspaper.

The Mrs (Queen of Sheba etc) has read in a mag somewhere that you need a horse, a sword and two sponsors to get in to the H of L. Alf from the allotments reckons she can have Dobbin the carthorse for the afternoon and we've got a sword from Geoff Cundell who found an old blade down the tip.

Can you sponsor the Mrs please M'Lud? There's a shop down Ealing Broadway called *Man at Lord Jon* where the Froggatt brothers (Ken and Sid) from no. 70 get kitted out for bowls club dos, so we thought we'd try them for the other M'Lud.

Hoping to hear soon.

Yours respectfully

RM Morello (Mr)

House of Lords
London
SW1A 0PW

4th June 2007

Dear Mr Morello,

I do see your difficulty and also the immense attraction for you of having the Mrs 'kicked upstairs.' There are indeed many in their Lordships House who have a lot to say for themselves but I am not entirely convinced that the Constitutional Committee of the Ladies Stoats Club has selected exactly the right candidate. The prospect of Mrs Morello arriving in a carriage complete with sword and newspaper might make good television but I fear that my fellow peers might never speak to me again.

I have another suggestion. There are discussions ongoing about the succession - Camilla and all that. In this democratic age there is another position which Mrs M. might like to apply for. The present incumbent is getting on a bit and may decide enough is enough and the rightful heir may just decide he would rather tend his organic garden and so, bingo, the post would be vacant. I could always absent myself from the State Opening and reappear when their Lordships had forgiven me.

What do you think of that idea?

Sincerely,

McNair.

Lord McNair.

Park View Road
Ealing
London W5

29 November 2005

Peter Stringfellow Esq
Stringfellows
16-19 Upper St Martins Lane
London WC2H 9EF

Dear Peter

Hoping all's going well with the Club!

Are you now doing round the clock boozing?

The wife (Rosetta) visited the Club recently when Irene from the hair salon had her hen do with you. The girls had a great night out.

You may have noticed them coming in, all dressed up as nuns and cheerleaders. The wife had an L plate and some feathers on for some reason. She wanted to dress as a pixie apparently, and weighs 15 stone.

I understand you were dressed up as a werewolf that night!

Irene tells me that the wife met a nice elderly Arabian gentleman. And also Marco from Milan. And Geoffrey, a retired headmaster.

The Mrs was so impressed by the whole experience that she wants to open her own club. She's teamed up with two of Tosti's friends, Julian and Desmond, who apparently know Melvin Gaylord at No. 7, whose made a few bob doing overtime down at Harvey's, the gents' outfitters in Ealing Broadway, and who apparently knows Stringfellows quite well. And some other clubs .

After a chat with the boys the wife reckons she wants to call her Club *Strongpillows*. I'm sorry about this but please bear in mind the Mrs is pretty hefty and can be a bit tricky to shift when she's settled but let us know if there's any problem etc.

Best wishes

Yours truly,

RM Morello (Mr)

34

Park View Road
Ealing
London W5

28 December 2005

Peter Stringfellow Esq
Stringfellows Club
16-19 Upper St Martins Lane
London WC2H 9EF

Dear Peter

I hope you had a Merry Christmas – and here's to a Happy New Year too!

I am just following up on the letter of 29 Novbr. which I hope you received safely – a
spare copy is attached. Mrs Morello was rather concerned as she hadn't heard
anything but I said you were bound to be esp. busy over the frestive season with
parties, hoggmanays etc and suchlike.

Plans are afoot for **Strongpillows,** which should be up and running quite soon. Would
you be able to attend the Grand Opening in February? Some major talents should be
attending, and Little and Large too.

Is it ok to advertise the new club at and around Stringfellows? We thought something
like:

Rosetta Morello, Julian and Desmond
<u>in association with Melvin Gaylord</u>

are delighted to announce the Grand Opening of their new venture

"STRONGPILLOWS"

From 8pm on 25 february 2006.

A host of entertainers will be present.
Peter Stringfellow might be there.

No chubs or uglies.
Or large bots.

Hoping you can attend to view the wife's opening.

Best wishes
Yours sincerely
RM Morello (Mr)

Park View Road
Ealing
London W5

28 December 2005

The Chief Executive
B and Q plc
Portswood House
1 Hampshire Corporate Park
Chandlers Ford
Eastleigh
Hants SO53 3YX

Dear Sir

I am Mr Morello and an Italian gent. The whole family think your stores are great –
and definitely better than Homebase and Trescos etc. We're popping in all the time.

Anyway me and Mrs Morello (Rosetta) have been running a little bakery business we
nicknamed *Bunions* which hasn't done that well. Mostly the wife is quite slow about
the place what with those ankles, and Sammy keeps getting lost in the sidecar.

Now we're opening a bar down Ealing Broadway called *"Morello's"*. We're inviting
allsorts to the opening including Irene Filcock, the Zieglers, Mr and Mrs
Stoddart, and Cliff Richard probably.

We're also lining up some guests for the Happy Hour where the whole emphasis
will be on an easy, fun, relaxed feeling with laughter and merriment. So we're
hoping to get Dirty Den, Jack Dee and Victor Meldrew (the wife's favourite).

The wife read in the Daily Mail re a gent up North whose got banned from all
your stores for being a bit grumpy and was also hit with a plank . Also a gent
who got kicked a couple of times, in the Trossachs area I believe, and then also
got booted out of all your stores.

We'd like to have them along and wonder if you could get them an invitatation
or give us their habitation. We could also re-enact all the fun you have with them,
especially as it's nearly Christmas.

Hoping to hear soon.

Many thanks for your help. Apologies for the poor English being Italian.

Yours sincerely,

RM Morello (Mr)

SP: have you got any trampolines that the ma-in-law, Annunziata (88), could try
out instore?

B&Q you can do it

Mr RM Morello
Park View Road
Ealing
London
W5 2JF

MIS123 / 8192-214851

13 January, 2006

Dear Mr Morello

Thank you for your letter dated 28th December 2005 in regards to your request for details of our trampolines, and information regarding guests for the opening of your new bar.

In regards to our trampolines, unfortunately they are a seasonal item, and as such are only available in the spring and summertime. Therefore more information will be available around Easter time from all our stores.

Regrettably, I must also inform you that we are unable to provide details of the two customers banned in store, mentioned in your letter, as this would be a serious breach of the data protection act.

I hope that these disappointments will not prevent you from shopping at B&Q stores in the future and thank you for taking the time and trouble to write to us. May I wish you all the best for the opening of Morello's.

Yours sincerely

B&Q plc Portswood House, 1 Hampshire Corporate Park, Chandlers Ford, Eastleigh, Hampshire SO53 3YX
www.diy.com B&Q is registered in England no. 973387

teamGB
Official partner

Park View Road
Ealing
London W5
29 December 2005

The Chairman
Burger King Limited
Charter Place
Vine Street
Uxbridge
Middlesex UB6 1BZ

Dear Sir

May I wish you and all your staff and customers a happy and prosperous New Year and long life.

I don't know about you, but I'm fed up to the back teeth with this constant carping about Burger King's burgers being bad for you. This is not my experience at all.

I and all my family (the wife, Rosetta, and the kids Tosti (17), Amphora (14) and little Rizzo (7)) have been scoffing your food for years, and I try to ensure we have a proper family meal round one of your tables at least three times a week. We love all your menu products. I try to see that the youngsters get a couple of Whopper JR's with cheese in the morning, followed by an XL Double Whopper and onion rings (large) whereas I and the Mrs go for a Rodeo Burger, or Supreme Cheeseburger (if the wife's fasting), with lashings of hash browns on the side. And a couple of Splurge with Twixels to round it off. Then we and the kids like to flush the whole lot down with a brace of Starburst Joosters (scrumptious) and a piping hot BKCoffee!

We also love the Ocean Catch, and the Diddy Donuts, (though I feel a bit of a t*sser ordering them when there are other customers around).

However we were quite taken aback on entering the Neasden branch recently. Cries of horror went up round the table, and lots of chubby little faces were castdown into dismay as they scanned the menu in vain for the Ultimate Breakfast and XXL Double Whoppers - only to find seared chicken pieces, crunchy baguettes and fruit juices!

Could you please explain this worrying trend to some of your most faithful customers, and reassure us this is a one off that won't effect our own outlets? We should be most grateful to hear shortly.

Whilst writing could you very kindly send us some careers information for young Tosti, who the wife believes would do well working in a local branch. The wife also enquires by the by whether staff discounts are available?

Yours sincerely

RM Morello (Mr)

18 January 2006

Ref # 192131

Mr. R M. Morello
Park View Road
Ealing
LONDON
W5

Dear Mr. Morello,

Thank you for your recent letter and for bringing this matter to our attention. I can assure you that whilst we currently have 'healthy options' on the menu, we will continue to serve your favourites*.

It is a pleasure to receive letters such as yours. We would like to assure you that Burger King® aims for the highest possible standards of food quality and service in all restaurants. Our operational procedures, and the training processes which all staff undergo are designed to protect and promote these high standards.

With regards to careers at Burger King®, I would be happy to forward you our Human Resources department contact details if required.

We hope your next visit will give us another opportunity to provide you with an enjoyable dining experience.

Yours sincerely,

Customer Careline

Enclosures: 4 Meal Vouchers
                1 Kids Voucher

*At participating restaurants, subject to availability, whilst stocks last.

END OF CORRESPONDENCE

BURGER KING UK & EIRE RESTAURANT SUPPORT CENTRE
Charter Place • Vine Street • Uxbridge, Middlesex UB8 1BZ
BurgerKing Limited. Registered Office: 242 West George Street, Glasgow G2 4QY. Registered No. 31456

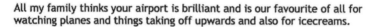

Park View Road
Ealing
London W5
30 december 2005

The General Manager
Southampton Airport
Southampton SO18 2NL

Dear Sir or Madam

All my family thinks your airport is brilliant and is our favourite of all for watching planes and things taking off upwards and also for icecreams.

Is it ok when I'm staying with nan if I take my new leopard Henrietta for a run most mornings round the perimeter fence of the airport, say about 9am till about 10 or something? She's dead fast and can overtake most things without even trying. She's really friendly when you get to know her and only nips people who seem scared.

Its only about an hour a day. The thing is they closed the Athletics Club near us and anyway it was getting a bit small. She could do the 400 meters in about 12 seconds. We could take her on a lead part of the time eg when she gets out of the back of the Fiat and gets her coat off and before she heads off.

Dad reckons it would be best if you stopped the planes running around while she's running incase it distracts the pilates who might bump each other slightly.

We won't just turn up for a run. We can fill in a form first if you want.

Thanks a lot for your help ect. Sorry if it causes any inconvenience on this occasion.

We used to take the giant leopard Lampard down the running club for a sprint. He even did the hurdles. But then he bashed something hanging down at the back between his legs and started howling like crazy and went and bit mum a bit when she was laughing at him and now she keeps him in the old pigeon shed most of the time though Dad reckons he should've got a medal.
Hoping to hear soon.
Yours sincelery
Rizzo Morello
Rizzo Morello (aged 7)

Southampton International Airport Limited

Southampton
Hampshire
SO18 2NL

BAA Southampton ◢

Rizzo Morello
Park View Road
Ealing
London
W5

13th January 2006

Dear Rizzo,

Thank you for your letter dated 30th December 2005 regarding exercising your new leopard Henrietta around the perimeter of Southampton Airport.

Unfortunately, Southampton Airport does not have a clear access route around the entire perimeter fence available for such purposes as you suggest. May I suggest that you contact Southampton Sports Centre, as they have a running track or alternatively one of the many parks situated in the London area.

Once again thank you for contacting Southampton Airport and I wish you luck in your search for running facilities for yourself and Henrietta.

Yours sincerely

Debbie Chalk
Communications Executive
BAA Southampton Airport

BEWARE OF THE PIGEONS

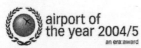
airport of
the year 2004/5
an era:award

INVESTOR IN PEOPLE

Registered in England 1990920 Registered Office 130 Wilton Road London SW1V 1LQ

MORELLO'S MENAGERIES

Park View Road
Ealing
London W5

1 January 2006

Sir Terence Conran
Bibendum
81 Fulham Road
London SW3 6RD
And by fax

Dear Sir Terence

Mrs Morello and I think that your restaurant Bibendum is a quite marvellous spectacle, and we believe leads the way as far as eating out and slurping great wine is concerned. The crustaceans and langoustines are renowned as superb. We also greatly admire you as the foremost innovative entrepreneur in this country's recent history.

We run a little menagerie and occasionally sacrifice some of the smaller animals for consumptive purposes. We have a small collection of rodents and intend to start a shop/restaurant quite near yours called **"Gerbilium"**.

The concept is a quite simple one – we shall be serving up rustic Sicilian recipes such as lightly toasted mouselet in a prawn batter with gerbil coulis; also gerbil surprise with hamster sauce and pine nuts.

But also we are planning some opening spectaculars. These involve window displays showing gerbils, hamsters and the rest fighting with various popular fish. They will enter combat in tanks with about an inch of water in them, so the fish can breathe but their rodent foe won't drown. In fact the rodents will be wearing tiny scuba outfits with flippers and snorkels.

But make no mistake – this is combat to the death.

We expect colossal crowds to witness :

Gerbil v Monkfish
Squid and bass combo v guinea pig
Hamster v Prawn and shrimp platter
Skate v stoat (grudge match).

The wife and I are hoping you will give this venture your blessing and be able to attend the Grand Opening later this month? You might be able to referee one or other of the contests.

Hoping to hear soon. Apologies that we're Italian.

Yours sincerely

RMMorello (Mr)

c/o Park View Road (PO)
London W5

31 December 2005

KGB Cleaning Group
Unit 5 Gun Wharf
241 Old Ford Road
Tower Hamlets
London E3 5QB

Dear KGB Cleaning Group

I wonder if you perhaps know something we don't, possibly?

I suggest we meet early in the New Year, in the park, on a bench. I will wear a trench coat and hat, and have a copy of The Times folded neatly beside me.

The day before we are due to meet you will see a notice in the Classified section of the Daily Telegraph reading *"Now is the time when the Thames will run from its very source out to the open sea. Box No: 3752"*.

I will introduce myself in the park as follows: *"They say the bluebirds fly too close to the sun in Springtime"*. I will then pass you an envelope. **Do not open it until you are back home, inside, with the door closed and the curtains drawn.** I will tip my hat and leave. Do not follow me. You will never see me again.

Be resolute. Be brave. The time is approaching when all will be well.

Please now eat this letter.

Yours in brotherhood

RM Morello (Mr)

PS: can you buff up the lounge carpet and throw in a once over on the kids' bedrooms, for about a ton or less?

MORELLO'S MENAGERIES

Park View Road
Ealing
London W5

7 March 2006

The Ambassador of Austria
18 Belgrave Mews West
London SW1X 8HU

Dear Ambassador

Please may I respectfully request some advice on a rather painful topic?

Last summer the wife and me were down the Acton Empire watching *Jaws II* which we'd chosen for our 20th anniversary (tin or lead or something). We were nicely settled into the Lower Circle loaded up with popcorn and a couple of toffee apples. On came a travelogue about holidays in Austria featuring a charming pastoral scene up a mountain with a load of milkmaids hanging around a cow and generally smiling and some blossom.

Suddenly a bloke in leather underwear strode on and started yodelling with full welly. Whether he was courting the young maids I'm not sure, though the cow moved away rapidly when he started crooning at full volume. The noise was quite colossal. The wife, smiling broadly at the screen, began vaguely murmuring the tune to herself throughout the rest of the ads (Pearl and Dean etc) – and right through the main feature, even where the shark nips that cable and gets electrocuted.

A couple of days later I noted Mrs Morello had purchased a Frank Ifield double album and was yodelling along. **Now she yodels non stop. This goes on even when she's mucking out the menageries in the back garden. But as soon as the strange discordant warbling strikes up all the creatures rush in terror to the backs of their cages, and huddle together protectively, screeching and howling.**

It's a sad sight to see rows of anxious eyes peering out from the gloom, with even the gorillas and kangaroos hugging each other. Once as the Mrs was yodelling whilst clearing out the muck from the ostrich pen, one of the flightless avians slipped past her and in a desperate bid for freedom made a dash for the end of the garden and the wide open spaces of the allotments beyond. The wife, though bulky, can really shift when needed. She flung herself dexterously at the bird's legs, caught him by the big toe, wrestled him to the ground, and dragged him crestfallen back to captivity. A horrible silence enveloped the cage for days afterwards.

As yodelling was invented in Austria can you suggest an antidote? Eg are there any reverse-yodelling classes I can send the Mrs to before the matter becomes entirely unmanageable with animal breakdowns etc?

Hoping to hear soon. Sorry we're Italian etc.

Yours sincerely

RM Morello (Mr)

THE AUSTRIAN AMBASSADOR   London, 8 June 2006

Dear Mr. Morello,

We have well received your letter and been pondering on how to respond, respectively be of help in this severe case of yodellitis.

On the one hand, I am pleasantly surprised that this part of Austrian culture is obviously spreading, even without Embassy intervention. On the other hand, we feel not responsible for such dire consequences of viewing a tourist ad. Also, we cannot offer any compensation in case of animal-yodelling and other disturbances.

There are, in my view, several thoughts and proposals that come to mind:

May be you could argue to her that yodelling is a pre-modern means of communication in mountainous regions only (including South Tyrol, Alto Adige, but also, I am told, the Andes), informing distant neighbours on impending weddings, warriors and avalanches. It is thus not fit for flat-landlers, for our globalised age and for alluring (or scaring off) lovers (including husbands) or animals, tame or wild. Due to modernisation, also in Austria, it is nowadays mostly practised on unsuspecting tourists. They mostly like it, or pretend to.

Have you considered that your wife may be doing this out of Freud (German for joy) and that she might subconsciously want to tell you something? Might

Mr. R.M. Morello
Morello's Menageries
Park View Road
Ealing
London W.5

AUSTRIAN EMBASSY, 18 Belgrave Mews West, London SW1X 8HU
Tel: +44 20 7344 3250, Fax: +44 20 7344 0292
e-mail: london-ob@bmaa.gv.at

she want to woe you like the lad in the ad, and has your reaction made her turn to quadrupeds instead?

Also, your wife may just dispose of an extraordinary natural gift in yodelling, since this art, mostly performed by men by the way, is anything but easy (you should try yourself). One yodeller alone is a sorry sight, it usually takes at least somebody to respond. So why not join her? That might make her stop.

As such natural abilities are surely rare your wife might want to join a yodelling group or attend a course in Austria (I shall find out which ones are on offer, if you are interested).

Alternatively she might want to found a "Yodellers Anonymous" in her neighbourhood. You might also consider an intervention by Animal Rights protectors, but not too robust.

Your being Italian has nothing to do with this late (confidential) response, rest assured.

Best regards,

Gabriele Matzner-Holzer

AUSTRIAN EMBASSY, 18 Belgrave Mews West, London SW1X 8HU
Tel: +44 20 7344 3250, Fax: +44 20 7344 0292
e-mail: london-ob@bmaa.gv.at

MORELLO'S MENAGERIES

Park View Road
Ealing
London W5
25 June 2006

Ambassador Gabriele Matzner-Holzer
The Embassy of Austria
18 Belgrave Mews West
London SW1X 8HÜ

Dear Lady Ambassador (or Gent, possibly)

Many thanks for your important letter re: yodelling in Austria dated 8 June which me and the Mrs have read several times on the kitchen table.

Sorry we don't know how to address you as there weren't many hints in the letter as to whether being a Gabriele you're a gent or could be a lady possibly not having met up etc. We had a vote on it and it was 3 all in the house (including our new lodger Robin Dovecote in the attic). So we asked some of the animals to vote they just had to point to a picture of a gent or a lady we showed them. Then it was 3-3 again, so Delia the gorilla voted and pointed to the lady picture. So that settled it and you're a Mrs. Ambassador. (Any chance of a pic signed for the wife's ma, Annunziata?).

We were quite interested, ma'am, in your bit about yodelling down valleys should there be an invasion or avalanche etc coming forth, which personally I preferred to the other bit about the wife wooing and reproducing herself with four legged creatures etc without me knowing. Anyway we're not flat-landlers as we live up a hill and consequentially cos we get trouble with the geriatrics from the Fairviews Old Folks Home round the corner shouting out when they get back from bingo Wednesday nights (*House! House!* Etc), the Mrs has been up on the roof yodelling quite loud by way of warning to neighbours down the road to shove in their earplugs etc.

Personally I reckon the Mrs' yodelling has got worse, and it's still upsetting the beasts esp Delia whose due for twins quite soon and gets right uptight as the Mrs shins her way up the drainpipe clearing her throat on Wednesday evenings.

Could you very kindly send us the brochure or whatever about yodelling in Austria like you said? Would it be possible for the Mrs to be sent there for quite a long time?

Hoping as the Ambassador you might become King or Queen of Austria one day so hoping to stay in touch.

Yours respectfully

RM Morello (Mr)

PS: Where exactly is Austria?

END OF CORRESPONDENCE

47

Park View Road
Ealing
London W5

25 March 2006

Des Lynam Esq.
C/o Countdown
Yorkshire Television
LEEDS LS3 1JS

Dear Des

I and my wife (Rosetta) have always loved **Countdown** and also adored you on **Match of the Day,** and reckon we're your biggest fans nationwide. In fact the Mrs is convinced we once saw you on the promenade at Brighton holding a 99 and a bag of chips. We would like to pose a small question.

Forgive us for being impertinent, but would you consider doing an edition of Countdown in the nude? Mrs Morello and I are keen naturists and it would give me and her (she has very painful feet) great pleasure if we could sit in our deckchairs in the back garden watching our favourite programme, whilst the presenters were staring back at us in the altogether!

I know this sounds odd but we really think it might work. Maybe for Countdown's 100,000th edition or whatever?

If you agree I also have some ideas of guests who might join you for this one-off, though Mrs Morello does not necessarily agree with all of my suggestions. I would probably have to write to you separately about this. Don't mention it to Carol at the moment.

I am very grateful for your time, and if you weren't so busy I'd ask you something else but feel I can't. Apologies for being Italian but hoping this won't stop you answering.

Sincerely yours

RM Morello (Mr)

PS: have you ever done an animal Countdown, with say a donkey pitted against a llama whom I believe are quite comparable intellectually on average? Don't bother about this question as much as the other one.

PPS: our second (Amphora, 14) thinks your "cute" and wants to ask for your photo but is too shy to write. Would this be possible please? I enclose an SAE for assistants.

Des Lynam

END OF CORRESPONDENCE

MORELLO'S MENAGERIES

Park View Road
Ealing
London W5

18 April 2006

Dominic Dromgoole Esq
Artistic Director
Shakespeare's Globe Theatre
21 New Globe Walk
Bankside
London SE1]

Dear Mr Dromgooles

Hello! I would like to introduce myself as Mr Morello. I am writing to you as an eminent scholar and researcher into the question of the Bard of England, sweet Swan of Avon etc, also known to/as Professor Sir Stanley Wells.

Whenever a new influx of creatures etc arrives at our menageries here we have a Grand Opening Ceremony involving as often as not a celebrity appearance to induct the beasts and make them homely and at ease surrounded by our kids and various other animales.

By the by the Mrs and me have just received delivery of a pile of new goats. They're quite a ragbag of critters involving Boers, pygmies, northern tufted straightbacks and a couple of quite rare Devon bluenecks.

But there's one particular beast that is unquestionably aside and apart from the rest. He's a superb specimen – tall, dignified, with a lovely white silky coat and long snowy beard. He stands aloof and magnificent in the stinging nettles in the corner of the garden, keeping his own counsel, silently surveying the daily scene unfolding about him with pale blue knowing eyes. Mrs Morello (Rosetta) and myself have had some heated debate about a suitable name for this paradigm. Despite disagreements (fur flying etc) we 've finally agreed the name should be........**Shakespeare.**

We're planning the animals' induction for **Sunday 21 May**. We realise it would be a long way to come and that you must be very busy, but the wife says we would be delighted if you would graciously consent to pop your head in to the goat's Opening.

We could of course collect you off the train at say Ealing Broadway or West Acton or even Hanger Lane and top you up with some sandwiches and a wagon wheel on the way home, and a toffee apple.

Hoping to hear soon. Thanks for your help.

Yours sincerely

RM Morello (Mr)

PS: The wife enquires whether you prefer sardine or fishpaste?

10 May 2006

SHAKESPEARE'S GLOBE
21 NEW GLOBE WALK   BANKSIDE   LONDON SE1 9DT
TEL +44 (0)20 7902 1400   FAX +44 (0)20 7902 1401
WEBSITE: www.shakespeares-globe.org

Mr RM Morrello
Park View Road
Ealing
London
W5

Dear Mr RM Morello

Thank you very much for inviting me to a goat's opening. Unfortunately I will be busy that day trimming my beard.

THE ST FINBARR'S RAMBLERS ASSOCIATION

Park View Road
Ealing
London W5

6 May 2006

George Melly Esq
c/o Ronnie Scott's Jazz Club
47 Frith Street
Soho
London W1D 4HT

Dear George

Please may I introduce myself. I am Mrs Morello and the Secretary to the St Finbarr's Ramblers Association (founded 1926). We are a group of like-minded folk of all sorts and ages who wander around the countryside singing and chanting happy songs about nature and birds etc, and picking a few flowers as we go, and herbs.

We love all of God's creation including fauna as well as flora, so this year we're introducing a few emus into the walks, and a couple of llamas or possibly a meerkat which one of our members recently inherited. **The emus will be led on a bit of string as they get nervous walking round lots of corners. So we're going to try to walk as far as possible in a straight line.**

We've got a packed programme this season, and you may be excited to know we'll be in your area **during a Sunday afternoon in May or June**. As we're starting out from the local railway station and going north north west, our Chairman has calculated that on the line taken the whole group expects to bisect your back garden, probably at around 3.15 to 3.45pm. We hope that's ok but if not hoping to hear soon and we can try to alter the route a bit, and experiment with little hoods for the emus. Several of our members, who are sun worshippers, like to walk stark naked (except for sandals and rucksacks), but can cover up if passers-by express a strong personal preference. No dogs allowed.

If you feel you would be interested in joining us on a ramble, or linking up with us as we trudge through your garden, do feel free. Please bring some stout footwear for comfort, and waterproofs. A modest contribution is requested. It would particularly joyful if you could bring a guitar and lead us in some of our songs as we all tramp along, or maybe just blast out a few tunes on your saxophone.

We have some nice packed lunch ideas, and help in getting your first Blue Peter badge.

Hoping to hearing soon.

Yours sincerely

Rosetta Morello (Mrs)

Hon Chairman: The Rt Rev Maurice Flambard DD MA
Hon Treasurer: Betty Trubshaw (Mrs)

GEORGE MELLY

Rosetta Morello   26th May 2006
Park View Road
Ealing
London W5

Dear Rosetta

Thank you so much for your courteous and kind invitation to join the St Finbarr's Ramblers Association to which I am afraid, for rasons I'll explain, I must decline.

At first I thought this might be a hoax letter sent me by someone who knows me well and is aware that I have been, since the age of 16, a convinced atheist. I have nothing against believers but wish no part in their activities except occasionally a donation to something Christian-run but for the relief of the starving, the politically persecuted, etc. However if this is a letter from your association, you will see my convictions stop me wandering around the countryside loving God's creation (the emus and llamas make me again suspicious that I have been sent a rather brilliant hoax).

I wish you well, if you're really there, in the enjoyment of the countryside. That at least I share. I would point out however that I cannot play a guitar nor the saxaphone.

Yours still in doubt

George Melly

George Melly

GEORGE MELLY is exclusively represented by:
Jack Higgins, Pear Tree Cottage,
Weymarks Farm, Bradwell-on-Sea, Essex CM0 7JB

Park View Road
Ealing
London W5
6 May 2006

Keith Porteous Wood Esq
Executive Director
The National Secular Society
25 Red Lion Square
London WC1R 4RL

Dear Mr Porteous Wood

I understand you are the head of a large and very successful atheist society, the NSS.

Please may I introduce myself. I am RM Morello and an Italian gent. I was once an atheist who didn't believe in God or any of His Works. However I became so disgusted about the permissive society and it's pervasive effect with respect to everything (TVs, microwaves, eclectic blankets etc) that I got rid of the lot and got involved in the druidical movement.

I gradually began to realise from first principles that there must be something in the "Godworshippers" as I had termed them. After all if no God exists around the place, how come we've got all these churches and bishops, and days off like Easter Sunday, Xmas Day and the rest (which apart from anything are a blessed relief from more shopping days etc). Then when I realised the strange things the druids get up to "Under the Oaks" as they put it, I reported them to the RSPCA and became a C of E. Anyway we met quite a nice bloke on holiday in Tenerife who turned out to be a bishop with a time share.

The final camel over the straw's back was a horrendous evening in Weymouth where me and the Mrs (Rosetta) were having a long weekend away from the kids. We were strolling along the foreshore on the promenade when we came upon a massive din outside the so called Ethical Hall. **What was going on was an almighty punch up between the atheists and the agnostics. This had spilled out onto the street, with bottles, fists and certain words flying around, a bit like the rods and mockers way back in the 1920s or whatever.** The whole scene was a disgrace, and in no way fitting for a responsible group of disbelievers (or uncertains). That said, the atheists acquitted themselves well and definitely got the better of their doubting opponents, who seemed somewhat non-committal and so left themselves vulnerable to sudden jabs and blows.

The modern church is by no means perfect in all its parts and as I regard myself as a bit of a freethinker, I would quite like to join your society whilst having half a foot in the Anglican world.

May I ask if there are any books you could recommend me and the Mrs to read in order to get attuned to secularism before we commit ourselves to a Godless world. We may need to do this gradually to avoid upset on the Parish Committee where Mrs Morello traditionally helps out with the Christmas bric a brac.

Many thanks, God bless

Yours sincerely

RM Morello (Mr)

national
secular
society

25 Red Lion Square
London WC1R 4RL
TEL: 020 7404 3126
FAX: 0870 762 8971
EMAIL: enquiries@secularism.org.uk
WEB: www.secularism.org.uk

Mr R. M. Morello,
Park View Road
Ealing
London
W5

12 June 2006

Dear Mr Morello,

Thank you for your letter. Keith Porteous Wood has asked me to deal with you – in the nicest possible way, of course - as he is far too busy taking care of the vast and increasing membership of the NSS at the moment and cannot be troubled with people who have one foot here and one foot there – stretched over a fence, presumably. First of all, we would like to say how thrilled we are that you are an Italian gentleman.

As for Druidism, I'm afraid I must refer you to our good friend, Rowan Williams the Archbishop of Canterbury (whom you'll be fascinated to learn is the son of the late, great Stanley Unwin, and is keeping up the grand family tradition of talking in a way that nobody can understand). Rowan is, of course, a Druid himself and is prone to going to Wales and waving branches about. He also recites what he calls "poetry".

I am sorry that you are so disturbed – in the sense of being alarmed by the fracas outside the Ethical Hall in Weymouth. I remember it well. I was in the forefront of the atheist contingent and managed to land a left hook to the jaw of Mr Harold Hornsey, a so-called "agnostic" who had created a schism in the movement in 1876 over the issue of Fair Trade tea.

You ask for book recommendations. I suppose Swallows and Amazons might be useful and the works of that lovely lady Evelyn Waugh are always diverting. I understand that there is some controversy at the moment among the Catholics about the Da Vinci Code.

Your letter brought to mind another marvellous correspondent we once had, a Mr Henry Root. I believe he's in an asylum now. Best wishes to you and your good lady wife (may we call her Rosetta?). Hope she doesn't burn her fingers while making jam for the church fete.

Yours sincerely,

J. L. Percival esq.

J.L. Percival.
Senior deputy assistant chief under secretary to Keith Porteous Wood

(END OF CORRESPONDENCE stamp)

National Secular Society (Company limited by guarantee. Registered in England No. 1418145)   Registered Office address shown above

Park View Road
Ealing
London W5
January 1st 2006

The Managing Director
The London Dungeon
28-34 Tooley Street
London SE1 2SZ

Dear Sir

Hello. My name is Derek Hardstaff MA (Oxon). I am a retired Deputy Headmaster. I believe in a firm, no-nonsense approach to life. Indeed it is this lax, shilly-shallying undisciplined attitude the young of today seem to show towards authority that has got our great country into this awful mess. The Conservative Party was at last seeming to get somewhere with its previous leader who promised a tough get-even policy with layabouts and all the ghastly vermin across the Channel. But now they've unceremoniously dumped him in favour of something little better than a raspberry ripple. I ask you!

Call me old fashioned if you will, but I believe the stocks, the strap and if need be, a moderate amount of flogging, can only do good for the nation's youth. Ask Nelson how he won the Battle of Trafalgar for God's sake? With flower arranging lessons and community service? Bah!

I am led to understand that your establishment is one of the few places left within these shores where discipline and respect for authority really stand for something. I should like to visit your premises with a view to permanent employment where I will be able to assist in the administration of appropriate levels of corporal punishment, canings and digital abrasions. I must make clear that I do this out of a sense of duty – another concept we all had knocked into us in my day but which in the modern era is all too often thoughtlessly scoffed at by the mindless do-gooders who control our media.

I shall arrive at 7am on Monday morning 16th January unless otherwise instructed. I will be fully equipped and will have the wiring and electricals ready-prepared.

I should add whilst at Eton I fagged for Major General Bullington-Smythe V.C., and that I have 25 years' experience in the Territorial Army (interrupted by a brief two year spell in hospital).

I am presently lodging in the spare room with a rather unsatisfactory family, the Morellos, at the above address, to which all communications may be directed.

Yours sincerely

D.R.St J. Hardstaff (Mr)

PS: I should like to enquire whether you get many Japs in?

NO REPLY

MORELLO'S MENAGERIES

Park View Road
Ealing
London W5
25 June 2006

The Ambassador
The Embassy of Ecuador
Flat 3
3 Hans Crescent
London SW1X 0LS

Dear Ambassador

I should like to congratulate you and the Ecuadorean people on your great showing in
the World Cup 2006 (football) in Germany. Me and Mr Morello and the kids have
just been watching the game v Englandd where you nearly smashed one or two past
Mr Robinson in goal at the far end and hit the cross bar etc. **Vamos Tricolor!** etc.

The whole household was lined up in rows in front of the Grundig to watch the
spectacle: in the first row the smallest creatures -- gerbils, stoats, some smaller chimps
and a few other things; then a row of dogs and cats and a couple of wolverines; then
several goats and the orang utan; then the llamas, an alpaca and Delia and Kenton
(gorillas); and at the back Angus (the bullock), the flightless avians and a couple of
water buffalo. Many were sporting different countries' colours. Anyway David
Breckham bent one in on the hour after a nutmeg on De La Cruz and a free kick. The
animals went wild, with mad howling and screeching and feathers everywhere as the
keeper sprawled across the goalmouth just too late and the ball trickled in, setting up a
quarter final thriller with either Hollandia or Portugal. (Breckham was sick just
afterwards, and all the animals calmed down a bit, with some mild chuckling).

But the creatures that went really bollistic when Inglaterra edged in front were the
four guinea pigs - hugging, kissing, hi-fives etc etc. Childish behaviour as they're all
adults anyway. I noticed they then went very quiet again when Lara lashed just wide,
and Placido Domingo or someone whacked the crossbar following an Ashley Cole
desperate intervention from nowhere.

**Then Tosti (our eldest) passed us a pic in the papers which could explain the
rodents' hysterics when England scored: it showed Ecuador's national dish –
flattened slice of g-pig popped in batter with a side salad and crunchy lettuce,
plus large fries.**

**Would we be able to supply the Embassy with guinea pigs for consumptive
purposes? They're top bred, eating only special Crufts-approved dogfood and
also top grains such as cornflakes, and Cheerios later on when they're off to the
salerooms? Being top class rodents they'd be ideal for Ambassadorial receptions
at Hans Crescent. Also, we could do some gerbils as small food (finger buffets
etc), perhaps on a stick with pineapple chunks etc?**

We'll send over a brochure if you'd like. We find the palomino guineas are the
tastiest. With a fried egg.

Hoping to hear soon. Please reply to me not Mr Morello who is somewhat backward
re menus, and he's away anyway. Apollogies with the Englis.

Yours respectfully

Rosetta Morello (Mrs)

Park View Road
Ealing
London W5
14 July 2006

The Top Editor
Cambridge University Press
Edinburgh Building
Shaftesbury Road
Cambridge CB2 2RU

Dear Sir or Madam

May I introduce myself as Mr Morello, and an Italian gent. I would like to raise a small observation which could become relevant with respect to the monetaries and related considerations.

The Mrs was recently at the dentist's for some major work on the front and rear molars. The wife always favours an early arrival for maximum consideration of the magazines lying around in the waiting area before you go next door to have your teeth dismissed etc. and hopefully to slip any good literatures in the handbag when no one's watching (making appointments etc).

During the pondering of the mags the Mrs spotted an ad with a retired police officer flogging awnings for the back garden which could overhang the chimps' cage and also be quite useful for the ma-in-law to slide down in the unlikely event she ever sets fire to her bedroom (again), due to her tobacco pipe igniting the blankets. But the small print (which the wife always reads to the end) shows the awnings coming in at about £300 each assuming you get the worst ones. Anyway the wife, whose in charge of spending the money, also wants some new curtains for the bedrooms, with a bit extra so the cutoffs can be used for Delia the gorilla, whose expecting twins in August and could do with some privacy.

Coincidentally the wife's been talking about finally publicating the family's life story. She's got the provisional title in mind of **"The da Morelli Code"**. She wishes it pointed out that this is: **an astounding family saga of romance, power, tragedy and greed, of dark ambition and heroic achievement, of amazing courage overcoming all the odds in a bid to establish the menageries that today proudly bear the family's name*, all set against the breathtaking background of Sicily, Sardinia, and Greenford Broadway.**

The story starts with Annunziata Manfredini (the wife's ma) coming downstairs one morning in her curlers in Sicily in about 1920 to find a strange lump of catsick on the kitchen floor. Convinced this is in the shape of an ancient holy grail, she sets off on a quest that will change her life forever (and the cat's). The pace quickens as the ma-in-law treks across Italy and Northern Europe on the quest for a grail, leading to ancient mummies, strange priests and a couple of dead sheep.

The wife, whose quite large anyway, has discussed the script with a few girls from the Acton Ladies' Stoats' Club and the reviews are coming in fast and thick:

"An astonishing tour de force. A triumph."

"Beautifully crafted prose. A superb cast of characters"

"Peerless. Nothing like the da Vinci Code, which I've never heard of."

We all feel this could be the big book of the 20th century or whatever. The Mrs hopes we can cash in, and I'd quite like to extend the ferret shed.

Do you reckon you could shift a few boxes of such a masterpiece? (Probably best to keep the Mrs out of the screen version – having fallen out of the ugly tree etc).

Hoping to hear soon. Apologies we're Italian etc.

Yours sincelery

RM Morello (Mr)

* the council points out the name might have to be changed in 2007 due to a complaint from *"Morello's Gelatos"* of Ruislip. And Stoke Poges.

CAMBRIDGE
UNIVERSITY PRESS

R. M Morello, gent.
   Park View Road
Ealing
London W5

The Edinburgh Building
Shaftesbury Road
Cambridge CB2 2RU, UK

www.cambridge.org

July 31, 2006

Dear Mr Morello,

Your letter of Bastille Day arrived and caused considerable amusement. Sadly, we cannot pursue this, as Cambridge does not publish fiction, or even faction, but I am sure that in due course your ferret shed can, and will, be extended, as the possibilities raised are clearly endless.

Apologies for this disappointing response to a very stylish and witty proposal, and best wishes for successful dissemination in due course,

Yours sincerely,

Richard Fisher
The Top Editor and Executive Director (Humanities and Social Sciences Publishing)

MORELLO'S CAKES AND FANCIES

Park View Road
Ealing
London W5

29 July 2006

Santa Pod Raceway UK
Airfield Road
Podington
Wellingborough
Northants. NN29 7XA

Dear Sir

The wife (Rosetta) is very interested in heading for the Santa Pod Raceway to do some serious drag racing, on Thursday evenings if possible. She's got some experience as she often delivers the cakes and buns from the sidecar on the BSA Bantam. She's also done a few high speed wheelies down Hanger Lane which she puts down to an accident what with jamming up the gears but which could be her playing up to the young mechanics at Frinton's Garage as she storms by with the fancies. She weighs in at 15 stone plus.

Anyway the wife got the Fiat 600 nudging 63 mph last weekend on the spin up to Beccles to see her friend Daphne Drawbridge (whose just retired with stress - as a tour guide from the National Trust). While it was stuck in first gear. This could be why the roof rack shook off, with the picnic hamper on.

The Mrs asks if she can wear her curlers and handbag as she rips up the track in the Monster Truck or Rocket Bike? She really reckons on becoming an ace Straightliner. **In fact after about 4 sherries at the Parish summer fete she told the Rev. Scrimshaw that she'd like to** *"burn some serious rubber and be the meanest straightlining bitch on the strip"*. **And then fell backwards over the hedge.**

The Rev, who was visiting from his own church at St Barbara's Windsor, made his excuses and departed immediately.

Could we borrow the Jet Car for a warm up around Ealing Broadway, otherwise we'll keep practising with the Bedford Rascal, though this seems to have slowed down a bit since we started storing the sacks of goat feed in the back.

Hoping to hear soon.

Yours sincerely

RM Morello (Mr)

Park View Road
Ealing
London W5

The Club Secretary
The Royal Blackheath Golf Club
Court Road
Eltham
London SE9 5AF

15 July 2006

Dear Sir or Madam

I believe you are quite an upmarket old golf club, hence the name. The Mrs and I love to clock a ball about the place and have considerable experiences.

Please can I apply for membership? I've got my own clubs (half set) and some quite nice gear, such as a couple of diamond knitted jumpers (Val Doonican etc) and tight slacks. And a mashie niblett. The wife's a bit hefty and slow but I'll always see that she stands back to let any jam building up behind play through.

As Mrs Morello's ankles are rather dodgy she has to have some support. We're still waiting for the guide dog to come through, so for the moment she gets about with Enoch, our guide goat that we brought up on the move from Devon. He's a plucky little scamp so you won't have any trouble with him galloping away across the fairways at the day's first yell of *"Fore!"*. He'll stand his ground like the best of 'em – he even copped one in the niagaras one time in the back garden and hardly flinched. All he needs is a bucket of carrots or dandelions, and we'll bring a shovel in the golf bag to clear up any mistakes that pop out on the way round the course.

Could you ping us over an entry form? We'll smack it back down to Court Road with the readies before the Hon. Treasurer's even hauled himself out of the clubhouse and into the Bentley. If you need references, me and the wife've done quite a bit of pitch and putt up the road at Hanger Hill Park, and there's always Ted Pegg who runs the Crazy Golf down by the pier at St Leonard's on Sea who'll wise you up on our talents down the years – even when we're half cut and loaded up with haddock 'n' chips and candyfloss.

Hoping to hear soon.

Yours sincerely

RM Morello (Mr)

PS: the wife enquires whether you do many socials
so we can get to know the locals?
Also is there a caravan park where we can pull up for the night?

THE CLUB HOUSE
COURT ROAD
ELTHAM
LONDON SE9 5AF

SECRETARIAT
020 8850 1795

FACSMILE
020 8859 0150

EMAIL
info@rbgc.com

www.rbgc.com

Mr R M Morello
Park View Road
Ealing
London
W5

19 July 2006

Dear Mr Morello

Thank you for your letter enquiring about membership of Royal Blackheath Golf Club.

As you so correctly surmise, we are indeed an old upmarket golf club but we also enjoy the reputation of welcoming a wide range of characters into membership. Your letter set out quite a lot about your golfing experience and it would be helpful if the Secretary of the Hanger Hill Park Pitch and Putt could endorse your playing ability. It would then save time and avoid the need for submitting three cards for handicap purposes.

There might be a slight difficulty with regard to Enoch, your guide goat, as there is a Club Rule excluding dogs. I am sure that we could explain that goats are not therefore excluded, but failing that, we could consider the practice – adopted for my own dog – of conferring Honorary Membership on the goat.

The next step would be to come up and meet some members – a well placed crème de menthe frappe can make instant friends.

If you find this letter encouraging please contact me so that we can arrange a membership interview for yourself and Mrs Morello. It might also be helpful to meet Enoch, in case we have to consider Honorary Membership.

Your query regarding the parking of caravans is timely in that our immediate Past Captain has his own caravan parked at the Club and I am sure would be able to give you a local insight into the 'travellers'.

I look forward to your response.

Yours sincerely

M J Miller
Secretary

CC: Captain, Lady Captain, Chairman of Membership

PROFESSIONAL
020 8850 1763

STEWARD
020 8850 1042

Park View Road
Ealing
London W5
22 July 2006

Mike Brown Esq
General Secretary
Amateur Football Alliance
55 Islington Park Street
London N1 1QB

Dear Mr Brown

The Old Rosettonians

Now the dust has settled on the World Cup 2006, with Italia yet again proving victorious over the Arghs, Frenches, Danes etc etc the Mrs (Rosetta) has been inspired to unveil her team for the oncoming season **which we're hoping you'll allow into your league.** It's quite a crack squad this year, with stiff competition for the top spots around the penalty area and goalie. Everyone's had to satisfy a strict residency requirement ie no more than 1.5 miles away 5 nights out of 7. Here's how they line up for the opening game (v West Hounslow Geriatric Warriors, away, on September 25), complete with individual mascots awarded by the wife from the cages round the back:

1   Barrie Delgado (ferret)
2   Jed Hamstring (camel – 2 humps)
3   Fenton Cheeseman (ocelot) (ringer- on loan from Marylebone Terrapins FC)
4   Morrie Needleman (rat) (sweeper)
5   Dudley Grocock (weasel/estate agent)
6   Sven Sundkvist (snow leopard)
7   Derek Whiplash (armadillo) (capt.)
8   Otis Faraday (cheetah)
9   Monty Fabriziano (giant gerbil)
10 Terry Hosepipe (TBA, poss sealion)
11 Sonny Lanzarote (gerbil – small)
12 Sub's bench: CK Fu Chen (squirrel)

Team masseuse: Melba Doublet (Ms).
Formation: 1, 2, 7

At a warm up last weekend the Mrs (15 and a half stone excluding handbag) was on the field against the Heston Tigers and took out 5 of the opposition in the first 43 minutes through a combination of headbutts, short arms and groin attacks. She's off for the rest of the season (before it's even begun). She said it was *"proportionate retaliation"* for Zidane's chest butt on Maserati in the World Cup Final. Keith Pringle from the St John's Ambulance Brigade made the mistake of questioning that on the basis there were no frogs in the Heston line-up. He was spotted a few minutes later nursing a broken nose by the hospitality tent.

Hoping to hear soon about the league placing.

Apologies we're Italian etc.
Yours respectfully

RM Morello (Mr)

AMATEUR FOOTBALL ALLIANCE LIMITED
(Affiliated to the Football Association)
55 Islington Park Street
London N1 1QB
Tel: 020 7359 3493
Web site: www.amateur-fa.com
Email: info@amateur-fa.com

PRESIDENT: W H Evans
CHAIRMAN : J R Wilson

Mr R M Morello
Park View Road
Ealing
London W5

Dear Mr Morello,

Absolutely no need to apologise for being Italian (or anything else for that matter).

I am glad to hear that her indoors has a an inspired team for the forthcoming season but sorry to hear that she will be starting the season with a suspension!

My own team will be playing in the vicinity in October and the tone of your letter suggests I should keep well clear!!

Yours sincerely,

Mike Brown
Chief Executive

24th August 2006

END OF CORRESPONDENCE

The Amateur Football Alliance Limited Telephone 020 7359 3493 Facsimile 020 7359 5027
Registered Office 55 Islington Park Street London N1 1QB Incorporated in England Registration Number 3957859
Directors: D M Dunn, W H Evans, W P Goss, J Maskell, J R Miller, W M Perks, A Robinson, M J Samuel and J R Wilson.
Company Secretary M L Brown

29 July 2006

Dr Jerry Lemler
President
Alcor Life Extension Foundation
7895 East Acoma Drive Suite 110
Scottsdale
Arizona 85260
USA
And by fax

Dear Dr Lemler

I have been recommended to write to you by the family of one of your satisfied customers as the world's leading cryogenic practitioner and pioneer to assist with a situation.

I 'd very much like to deep freeze Mrs Morello for Christmas. My understanding is that usually your patients are deceased when lowered into the vats but in this case we believe it could be beneficial to accelerate matters if you deem this to be ethically acceptable and after ensuring all medical safeguards are in place.

I imagine the vats come in different sizes and I'd like to order an extra large.

I can be available to assist the wife over the edge though it may be necessary to stun her so I'll bring some large bricks along (wrapped in a towel for discretion).

We'd like to wake her up about Easter 2020. I'd expect she'll have forgotten about the situation with the bricks by then.

The Mrs may wish to take her handbag in with her. Hoping that's ok.

Look forward to hearing soon with your terms and a brochure.

All the best

Yours sincerely

RM Morello (Mr)

ALCOR LIFE EXTENSION FOUNDATION
7895 E. Acoma Dr. #110, Scottsdale, AZ 85260-6916

● www.alcor.org

Alcor's Mission: The Preservation of Individual Lives

29 July, 2006

RM Morello
Park View Road
Ealing
London W5

Dear Mr. Morello,

Re your fax, there are several immediate questions:

What is Mrs. Morello's condition? You hint at some urgency.

What is your relationship to Mrs. Morello?

If you have Web access, you can get information about us at
http://www.alcor.org

If you wish to make membership arrangements with Alcor, email Diane Cremeens at
diane@alcor.org

Sincerely,

Hugh Hixon

Park View Road
Ealing
London W5

30 July 2006

Hugh Hixon Esq.
Alcor Life Extension Foundation
Suite 110
7895 East Acoma Drive
Scottsdale
Arizona 85260
USA
And by facsimilator

Dear Mr Hixon

Many thanks for your rapid response to my fax letter of yesterday.

We've been having the devil's time here what with everything going wrong, and off, and realise it's something of a race against time (*"Tempus fugit"* etc). But everyone's so kind including Enoch, Desmond, Delia and the rest, who're almost like members of the family.

Thank you for your questions. In answer, I can only say that Mrs Morello's condition has been completely unsatisfactory for some time. She has after all been overly portly for as long as anyone can remember, and has had walking difficulties which, again, Enoch has been so helpful with.

Also my relationship with Mrs Morello has been ok thank you, but now I just wish I'd been with her more, instead of spending so much time on my correspondence etc. I suppose in the circumstances that's only naturalistic.

Unfortunately we don't have a web here in Ealing. I thought the telefax would be pretty quick to move things quite fast towards the vats, possibly.

Can I send you or Diane some monetaries now and we can get signed up and get the tricky bits over and move on to the better bits?

Thank you again for your attention. I look forward to hearing quite shortly.

Yours sincerely

RM Morello (Mr)

ALCOR LIFE EXTENSION FOUNDATION

7895 E. Acoma Dr. #110, Scottsdale, AZ 85260-6916

www.alcor.org

Alcor's Mission: The Preservation of Individual Lives

To: RM Morello

Mr. Morello,

We are sorry to hear of Mrs. Morello's condition. In order that we can better assess whether it is possible for Alcor to assist her, please call me at your earliest convenience at 001-430-905-1906, extension 113.

If you have not already, I recommend you contact another cryonics organization in the United States, Cryonics Institute (001-586-791-5961) They are more likely to accept Mrs. Morello's case than the Alcor Foundation.

Regards,

Jennifer Chapman
Membership Director

69

Park View Road
Ealing
London W5

31 July 2006

Ms. Jennifer Chapman
Membership Director
Alcor Life Extension Foundation
Suite 110
7895 East Acoma Drive
Scottsdale
Arizona 85260
USA
And by tele-facsimilator

Dear Ms Chapman

I am very grateful for your telefax letter received earlier today.

The whole situation with Mrs Morello has been a disaster for ages. It's so nice to be able to describe the position to someone after so long without worries about recriminations etc. and to feel that, in slowly lowering the wife into the freezing vat, we're not doing anything wrong even though we feel a great sense of relief and satisfaction. And pleasure.

We all find it rather difficult to speak about the Mrs' condition at this stage but I can confirm that she's definitely been kept pretty cold for a while. In fact I was out at Tresco's with Patrick and Enoch getting more lumps of ice and a polar hammer when your fax arrived. It's all under control but hoping to get the show on the road pretty soon.

In my view, and Delia and Kenton's, your suggestion that we consider another life extension agency is an example of your sound professional standards. Having gone straight to the top we are committed to seeing this interesting project through to the end - with the Alcor Life Extension Foundation. **We shall not feel safe until Mrs Morello is firmly esconced in her personal vat, secure for the future.**

Delia is expecting twins in November and so is quite sensitive to the situation, and explained that she was particularly touched by your comments.

I'm arranging the spondulicks and Mrs Morello will follow on shortly thereafter, after we've filled in the forms. Do you have a special vat suspension form and any guarantees? These could be about future recoveries or about a minimum period before resuscitation possibly?

Thank you again for your kind understanding.

Yours sincerely

RM Morello (Mr)

ALCOR LIFE EXTENSION FOUNDATION

7895 E. Acoma Dr. #110, Scottsdale, AZ 35260-6916

www.alcor.org

Alcor's Mission: The Preservation of Individual Lives

To: RM Morello

Mr. Morello,

We were not aware that Mrs. Morello is not still living. It is not Alcor's policy to accept cases of this nature. I recommend you contact another cryonics organization in the United States, Cryonics Institute (001-586-791-5961).

Best Regards,

Jennifer Chapman
Membership Director

Park View Road
Ealing
London W5
8 August 2006

Ms. Jennifer Chapman
Membership Director
Alcor Life Extension Foundation
Suite 110 7895 East Acoma Drive
Scottsdale
Arizona 85260
USA
And by faxsimilator

Dear Jennifer

Thanks so much for your further letter, received yesterday via the fax machine (now in a box under the stairs).

Could I just clarify that it would not be exactly right to refer to Mrs Morello as not living ie an exaggeration although she had to be kept cold during the extreme heat we experienced here in London over the past couple of weeks.

I am very grateful, so are Delia and Kenton, and Desmond and Enoch, for your kind advice about your rival The Cryonics Institute, though we have all discussed it and think The Alcor Life Extension Foundation would be best, especially as we know how strongly one of your patients recommends it.

Also, we saw Regina Pancake, your Head of Stabilisation Team, on the goggle box the other night here in Europe and thought she spoke excellently, and at one point was quite convincing.

I wasn't sure from Ms Pancake's address on a couple of points. Has anyone ever recovered from the treatment, Desmond enquires? Also can you be brought back at a different time from when you first thought you might, or would it depend on when your family think it would be best eg to do with whether they want you back and jobs etc? Eg could the family direct that Mrs Morello remain in the bottom of the vat with the lid firmly on even if your doctor could arrange her resurfacing?

Sorry about these follow-ups but it's a big decision given Mrs Morello's situationals.

We may well have some other clients for you. (Mr Schneider at No.26 is particularly interested in the deepfreeze programme for Mrs Schneider. He was down the building society last Tuesday).

Have the spondulicks arrived?

With best wishes

Yours sincerely

RM Morello (Mr)

PS: we should be over on 16 August about 1400 hours and will check in at the Travelodge before rolling up to inspect the vats (and lids). They were very good at Milton Keynes when we booked Kenton and Maureece in for the Chipperfields weekend.

MORELLO'S LOOKALIKES AGENCY (estd. 1973)
"Make Mine a Double"

Park View Road
Ealing
London W5
11 February 2007

The Rt Hon Gordon Brown PC MP
Chancellor of the Exchequer
11 Downing Street
London SW1

Dear Mr Brown

Mrs Morello and I are keen observers of the political scene and like to keep a close eye on key developments. The wife informs me that there are quite distinct opportunities for you to become the next PM (Prime Minister) after Mr Blair has finished with it.

Here at *Morello's* we run one of the most respected agencies in the country supplying look-alikes, sound-alikes and impersonators for busy professionals in public life with bulging diaries. If you do go for the top job there are several advantages to having a professional double:

1 ideal for meet 'n' greets, fundraisers and cocktail parties.

2 if in due course you were to become a celebrity there will be lots of events you'll attend where many guests won't recognise you anyway. Various meetings with say the Ambassador of Lesotho or the Chairman of the National Transport Board of Wales can be instantly struck from your schedule, confident in the knowledge that we at *Morello's* will cover it and no-one will notice the difference.

3 a double will save you time, cost and anxiety. If it goes well – Mum's the word, but if everything goes pear-shaped you can let it slip out that it wasn't you anyway. Few people know that several times over the past 10 years Tony Blair has been "represented" by a carefully crafted double - and not an eyelid was batted. Twice the stand-in was Bruce Forsyth. Even the speeches went quite well, till the end bit to do with the prizes.

We already have some doubles lined up for you. One is Robbie Coltrane. But, if you're on a tighter budget, I would also like to suggest Alexei Sayle.

Mrs Morello strongly recommends our special Diamond Service:

* 24/7 round-the-clock cover, including speech-writing assistance
* just 2 hours notice needed to wheel out a double
* special cover for difficult and notorious events eg The Women's Institute.

Hoping to hear soon.
Yours sincerely
RM Morello (Mr)

NO REPLY

73

MORELLO'S MENAGERIES

Park View Road
Ealing
London W5
19 August 2006

The Lord Mayor of Sheffield
The Lord Mayor's Office
The Town Hall
Sheffield S1 2HH

Dear Your Highness

I am Mr Morello, an Italian gent. I quite often visit the town/city/hamlet of Sheffield which I love – it's a brilliant place, sometimes with some of the beasts too including Enoch (goat), Neville (ferret) and Desmond (the lame emu), and Mrs Morello (Rosetta).

You can get a cheap day return from St. Pancreas for about twenty quid all in and Desmond comes in the guards' van where they quite like him and often give him a Twix or a possible Curly Wurly and a Marathon and he's allowed to stick his head out the window as the train whistles through all the stations at about 210mph. He once had a Marlborough Lite, which made his eyes water.

The other half (three quarters) likes to ponder the shop windows and bits and bobs of the town etc with her handbag and with Desmond and hangs around in estate agents for a bit of a chat and some cups of tea whilst inspecting other people's houses (without buying any); then on to Trudgwick's Department Store (Ladies Garments – 4th Floor) to try on some monstrous clothes. I've noticed she usually rounds off at Aunt Betty's Tea Rooms with an apple puff and a few fondant fancies. Or a cream horn.

Meanwhile me and the quadrapeds prefer the parklands and Enoch does some grazing etc and we talk to people who are quite nice sometimes. And we do some shopping and I like to inspect the recycling centre so does Neville who gets stuck in etc.

Is there somewhere you can get a good pop-up toaster around Sheffield? 4 slice **not** two slice and where you can remove the bottom without some complicated toolkit to expel the crumbs etc that get clogg'd up in the bottom. (From the bread that's gone in before).

Mrs Morello desires that we meet up quite soon in the Mayor's Parlour and she can wear a new hat and her unusual scorpion brooch. Could we come on say 3 September at about 2.30pm?

Hoping to hear soon. I wasn't sure who to write to etc.

Yours sincerely

RM Morell
RM Morello (Mr)

PS: Our old toaster had an accident and's been playing up, ever since Kenton backed onto it in the kitchen whilst preparing a tuna bap. We weren't certain whether to mention this bit.

Lord Mayor's Office

Town Hall, Sheffield, S1 2HH

25 August 2006

Signore R M Morello
Park View Road
Ealing
London   W5 2JF

Dear Signore Morello

Thank you so much for your letter dated 19 August.

I would have been delighted to welcome you and Mrs Morello on 3 September as I feel we would have such a lot in common. I too think Sheffield is a brilliant place to live, work and visit, and the shops happen to have an exceptionally good range of 4-slice pop-up toasters to choose from. Personally, I have to make do with a 2-slice, which takes twice as long, as my in-laws gave it to me as a wedding present. (I don't worry about the crumbs clogging up in the bottom. I just leave them in to burn as it makes sure everyone gets up for their breakfast when the smoke alarm goes off, without me needing to shout up the stairs.)

Unfortunately, I will not be here to meet you on 3 September as I will be having a day out in Italy. As you will know Pope Benedict XV, who was born in Italy, was made Pope on that day in 1914 and I always go to Italy in tribute when it falls on a Sunday. I can get a cheap flight from Doncaster Sheffield Robin Hood Airport; gaze at the art works of Botticelli, Leonardo da Vinci and Michelangelo; ride on a gondola; have a pizza and an ice cream; call in at the Vatican, watch one of Verdi's operas, and be back in Sheffield in time to make toast the next morning.

It is a shame about Mrs Morello's new hat and brooch though, as I always dress to impress and never appear in public without a big hat, even when I go out to hang the washing. I would suggest to Mrs Morello that she still wears them for the benefit of your menagerie, as I am sure that they will appreciate her making the effort.

Yours sincerely, *all good wishes*

Ciao Jackie or 'Lord Mayor' to you!

Councillor Mrs Jackie Drayton
LORD MAYOR OF SHEFFIELD

PS It is flattering for you to think of me as belonging to the realms of "Your Highness" but I am afraid I am a much lowlier "The Right Worshipful". As we are now literary acquainted, there is no need to be formal and you can simply address me as "Lord Mayor".

Telephone: (0114) 273 4025   Fax: (0114) 273 5037
E-mail: lordmayor@sheffield.gov.uk

Park View Road
Ealing
London W5

8 September 2006

Mr Paul O'Grady
17-19 Bedford Street
London WC2E 9HP

Dear Mr O'Grady

Hello! I'm Mr Morello and an Italian gent.

Me and the Mrs (Rosetta) love Liverpool. It's a brilliant place, a great cultural centre, Home of the Rolling Stones etc. We especially love Liverpool Zoo. Back in the 70s we did an amount of our courting around the zoo, especially near the big cats' cages, including the lions and the elephant seals.

Anyway the wife and me went back to Liverpool and the zoo on a sort of second honeymoon a couple of years ago. We were very pleased to see some familiar faces, including a really gnarled old beast that growls at every one as they enter the zoo, and roars with fury if anyone drops some litter. (I think that's Mrs Simpkin whose still working in the ticket office).

Anyway, we were somewhat disappointed to note that **several of the beasts have picked up a distinct nasal Scouser accent down the years.** We thought that might be off-putting and a little frightening for our kiddies should they visit with us on a return trip.

Here's just hoping you could write a small note that we could pass on to the zoo asking that they hide the beasts concerned when we roll up with the kids on October 2nd, about 11am. The culprits are:

the orang utan
the manatee
the lemur (Large)
the biggest hippo
the mountain goats (**all** of them)
and, worst of all......**the hyenas, all of whom seem to have developed a ghastly guttural twang when both speaking and laughing.**

Hoping you can help us keep the offenders under wraps for a few hours.

Look forward to hearing before the trip.

Apologies we're Italian etc.

Yours sincerely

RM Morello (Mr)

END OF CORRESPONDENCE

MORELLO'S MENAGERIES

Park View Road
Ealing
London W5
17 September 2006

The Right Honorable Christopher Patten Esq CH , The Lord of the Barnes etc.
The Chancellor of Oxford (University)
University offices
Wellington Square
OXFORD OX1 2JD

Dear Your Highness

Hello! I am Mr Morello and an Italian gent. I run a small but well-stocked menagerie here in Ealing with mammals, ruminants, gastropods, rodents, pond life and also the wife (Rosetta).

Me and the Mrs have recently extended the running areas, and find an immediate improvement in the general social skills of the beasts with respect to the communications and general civility of the critters. The qaulity of the scales and fur has rocketed (upwards) and the animales seem more relaxed and at ease with themselves (and each other, in the social setting).

We noticed you have to wear robes etc when going off to work as Chancellor. Mrs Morello (who is surprisingly bulky) wishes to offer to reline the interior which could have been worn out by previous elderly inhabitants, older and larger than yourself. **She wishes it to be known that we have some superb new alpaca fur in which is silky soft and snug in the winter, but cool and breathing-nicely for the summer collection, similar to the noble llama but nicer and speciall offers till Christmas . Ideal for Kong Hong should you return.**

By the by the other half is convinced we were previously acquatinted with yourself some years ago. It was at the Betty Trask Tea Rooms in Harrogate. You asked to borrow our butter dish, to do a trick with a bread roll, 2 spoons and a gerbil, which disappear'd, then popp'd up in Colonel Frobisher's breast pocket somewhat crazed and the Col. had a murmur, as did the tiny rodent which later was ok. The Col. removed to Scarborough's renowned Home for Elderly Officers Etc. and after some treatments was restored to the south and discontinued..

Could we visit with Kenton and Delia to measure up, say on 9 October at 2.45pm? We could meet up at Fandango's, the new place down the Cowley Road, which the wife advises does afternoon cocktails, and dancing til dawn.

Mrs Morello says we'll chuck in a badger for the trim if the deal's on.

Hoping to hear soon. Apologies we're Italian etc.

Yours sincerely

R Morello (Mr)

PS: We've got some more reasonably priced furs eg stoat and ferret, (or even gerb) if you're still doing gigs up in Newcastle

HOUSE OF LORDS
LONDON SW1A 0PW
15th May 2007.

Dear Mr. Morello,

Thank you very much indeed for your letter.

It was very kind of you to get in touch with me.   My gown at Oxford is not in fact lined with fur so I think your beautiful addition to a Chancellor's robe will have to surface elsewhere.

Best wishes,

Yours sincerely,

Dictated by Lord Patten and signed in his absence

END OF CORRESPONDENCE

Mr. R.M. Morello,
Park View Road,
Ealing,
London,
W5.

MORELLO'S MENAGERIES

Park View Road
Ealing
London W5
17 November 2006

Head of Customer Services
Good Energy Limited
Monkton Reach, Monkton Hill
Chippenham
Wiltshire SN15 1EE

Dear Sir, or Madame

Hello! I'm Mr Morello and an Italian gent.

Please can you help respecting some incidents to do with electricatory supplies regarding the domestic situation at home ref a rival which has supplied the electrics through the plugholes??

Last Saturday evening the Mrs (Rosetta) was mucking about with the electric sandwich maker. She was brassed off at the time as Prof Braintree from No. 32 had just complained (again) ref the noise concerning the tamarinds in the main menagerie shed who are quite noisy due to seasonal mating displays with full howling etc. The wife, whose not that delicate anyway (15.5 stone minimum, excluding handbag) evidently took the view the Breville needed some punishment, banging it on the kitchen table.

Then she plugged it in beside the toaster (4 slicer). There was a huge bang and a crackle. The sandwich-burner belched out a puff of smoke, and fell ominously silent. But suddenly the fishtank in the lounge started fizzing. Then one of the crested Ceylonese guppies only went and shot out of the tank, flew in an arc through the air, and landed in a glass containing granmamma's false teeth while the old bird, 88 (two fat ladies) snoozed beside it in the rocker.

Unfortunately at this precise moment there was a scream from an upstairs bedroom where our second (Amphora,14) was using her hairdryer on the barnet whilst getting it together for a first date at the Acton Young Fishmongers' Autumn Dance and Drugfest with Ivan Stankovic (17). Evidently some slight pyrotechnics happened there too what with the kid departing the house with the strange Croat with her hair looking like Don King on ecstasy (slightly crazed etc).

Anyway, since then every time the phone rings the garage door opens and closes. And whenever the doorbell sounds the wife's drawers fall down!

Can your service engineer come and look into the matter? We reckon the electricity we've been getting could be faulty (possible cheap foreign imitations etc). Do you do gas as well which could lead to less explosions esp if it's English or Ital.possibly

Hoping to hear soon. Apollogies for the use of Inglis, which is better than the wife's anyway.
Yours affectionately

RM Morello (Signore)

PS: Several of the animales were scared witless about the explosions, and the anteater's still stuck up the chimney etc. It wasn't definite we were going to mention this bit necessarily.

Good Energy ○

Mr R M Morello
Park View Road
Ealing
London
W5 2JF

Monkton Reach
Monkton Hill
Chippenham
Wiltshire SN15 1EE

6 December 2006

Dear Mr. Morello,
Subject: Morello's Menageries

Thank you for your letter dated the 17th November 2006. I am sorry to hear about the recent difficulties you have experienced with your electricity supply. As we are not currently the suppliers of your electricity, we wouldn't be able to send an engineer to check your metering set up.

It is more than possible that you are using a low quality grade of electricity. I can guarantee that if you were to switch your supplier to Good Energy, we will supply you with only the very finest electricity generated entirely from renewable sources. As the only company in Britain to offer this service, you can be sure that our electricity is of a much higher caliber then any other electricity supplier. I have enclosed one of our information packs, for your convenience.

I notice that you are using a lot of very energy intensive appliances. May I suggest that you take advantage of the open fire that you have (once you have extracted the anteater of course – we couldn't advocate animal cruelty)? There's nothing better then toasting your own sandwich over a roaring flame and I'm sure your daughter would experience a far less dangerous grooming regime sat in front of a calming fire to dry her hair?

I trust that I have been of some assistance to you. If you have any further queries, please do not hesitate to contact one of our Customer Service Team on 0845 601 1410. We would be delighted to hear from you.

Yours Sincerely

Michelle Howard
Customer Services Manager

81

MORELLO'S MENAGERIES

Park View Road
Ealing
London W5

1 January 2007!

Ms Michelle Howard
Customer services Manager
Good Energy
Monkton Reach
Monkton Hill
Chippenham
Wiltshire SN15 1EE

Dear Ms Howard

Hello! It's Mr Morello again and Happy New Year to you and all yours and the boss and colleagues as well and all of theirs, for the New Year (207).

Thanks a lot for your lettre of the Decr. 6th with the pack, which Enoch was interested in and he consummated that too after his normal breakfast.

Could we borrow some of your electricity to try out as it seems quite good compered to the other imitation stuff we've been using that has caused some experiences around the household. It might work better than the quantity we had from the other lot.

We could collect it in the Bedford Rascal next week as we're down near Wiltshire returning faulty llama with the Safari park. Or the Fiat 600 depending on the MoT situation.

Should we bring some crates and maybe a couple of barrels to collect it? If you could include some Italian electricity (say about 20 per cent) that would probably work best and we'll keep the beasts away from the containers on the return trip.

Do you do gas as well as the parrots find the hissing quite soothing in the sheds, and the snakes.

Hoping to hear soon

Yours respectably

RM Morello (Signore).

Good Energy ◯

Mr R M Morello
Park View Road
Ealing
London
W5 2JF

Monkton Reach
Monkton Hill
Chippenham
Wiltshire SN15 1EE

29 March 2007

Dear Mr. Morello,

Subject: Morello's Menageries

Thank you for your letter dated the 1st January 2007. 2007; just like 2006 only with a different number at the end.

Please find enclosed a small sample of Good Energy for your pleasure. We have charged this battery with 100% pure, clean renewable energy. I understand that this is particularly good for the television remote (unlike the Italian electricity, I understand the language settings can be affected by a faulty batch).

I am pleased to hear that Enoch found a good use for the information that we sent you. May I suggest that you discourage him from 'consummating' the enclosed sample if at all possible? Although this is only a small sample, electricity is dangerous and should not be toyed with.

Good Energy does not supply gas at present; renewable gas being a bit of a contradiction in terms. Perhaps you may consider branching into this industry yourself? With the volume of animals you keep you could use their dung for your own Biogas generator?

Please let me know if there is anything further I can do to assist you.

Yours Sincerely

Michelle Howard
Customer Services Manager

83

Park View Road
Ealing
London W5

28 November 2006

Stuart Rose Esq
The Chief Executive
Marks and Spencer Group plc
Waterside House
35 North Wharf Road
London W2 1NW

Dear Mr Rose

I am the Secretary of the Sunnyfields Sun Club (formerly Ealing Valley Sun Club) which is a nice little naturist members' society in Ealing.

Here at Sunnyfields we are rather better than the average naturist organisation in that we attempt wherever possible to bring the nudist way of life out into the open and so spread the message of peace, happiness and understanding in what, even now in the 20th century, is still largely a textile world.

I am charged with organising this year's Club Christmas outing. After a poll of members we would very much like to attend one of your stores, perhaps Ealing Broadway, for a **naturist shopping evening**. We would be happy to attend at a time when the store is relatively quiet so as to be as unobtrusive as possible to begin with.

Perhaps we could visit on say Thursday 14th December, aiming to arrive at about 5.30pm? There will probably be about 30 of us. We shall all be wearing shoes and possibly hats as well but otherwise we'll be fairly recognisable.

Hoping that's alright. Do encourage your staff to join in with us in what we believe could be a first in modern British retail. If you yourself would like to participate please rest assured we shall do all we can to make you feel relaxed and at home during the shopping experience.

It would be appreciated if you could raise the temperature a notch or two in the store from about 4pm as it could be quite chilly in the circumstances.

If there are any guide dogs etc around could they please be kept out-of-store during the proceedings.

Many thanks for your help – looking forward to the 14th.

Yours sincerely

Rosetta Morello (Mrs)

7 December 2006

Waterside House
35 North Wharf Road
London W2 1NW

Tel: 020 7935 4422
www.marksandspencer.com

Mrs Rosetta Morello
Park View Road
Ealing
London W5

Dear Mrs Morello,

Thank you for your letter.

The South Ealing Naturist Club is well known to me as I was Chairman between 1957 and 1959. My body was, at that point, toned and tanned. Time has not been kind to me since. My physique (and my mind) have deteriorated and for these reasons I am afraid I must decline.

with all best wishes
Yours sincerely

Stuart Rose
Chief Executive

PS: I may be King of the M&S Castle, Master of the Bra Universe, the Obi Won Kenobi of Fresh Fruit but I look back on those days in Ealing, when I could walk down the High Street, naked as the day I was born, feeling free and natural. Heady times indeed.

Marks and Spencer plc
Registered Office:
Waterside House
35 North Wharf Road
London W2 1NW
Registered No. 214436
(England and Wales)

MORELLO'S MENAGERIES

Park View Road
Ealing
London W5

12 January 2007

Stuart Rose Esq
The Chief Executive
Marks and Spencer Group plc
Waterside House
35 North Wharf Road
London W2 1NW

Dear Mr Rose

Hello. I'm Mr Morello, husband of Mrs Morello (Rosetta). The wife wrote to you last Nov and you wrote back on 7 December pointing out your nudist tendencies in the old days and mentioning some other things.

Thanks a lot for your letter. We're sorry you can't attend a naturist shopping experience at your Ealing Broadway store. The Mrs did have great hopes. Anyway she's convinced this is because you wear BHS underwear and socks which aren't much good as they're mostly terylene and can cause electric shocks to the toes and legs and possibly higher but Every Little Helps as they say.

Although he'd very much be the second choice, we might try Sir Philip Green for the nudist evening at one of **his** shops. **There are some natural drawbacks to this plan to do with the disrobing but if the BHS customers generally wear terylene they'll be used to shocks anyway when they see what's hit them on the night as Sir PG's gear comes off innit.**

The wife reckons she could meet up with you for a power breakfast to discuss the plan. We can meet at Sunnyfields, or at the menageries and the Mrs can wear her unusual new scorpion brooch. Or at lunchtime after some cocktails. The Mrs always feels better in herself after 5 or 6 crème de menthes. Shall we say Thursday 25th Jan at 12.30pm?

Hoping to hear soon.

All the best

Yours sincerely

RM Morello (Signore)

PS: the Mrs says we could even play a little trick on Sir Green maybe involving one of the beasts from the menageries – we don't want him outwitting you by stealing your position with respect to the nudist event. Possibly something that bites slightly.

MOLERRO'S MENAGERIES

Park View Road
Ealing
London W5

28 May 2007

The Senior Manager
Japan Letting Agency
177 High Street
Acton
London W3 9DJ

Dear Sir

We approach you as one of London's leading and best regarded property agents.

Mrs Molerro, whose the brains of this operation though no oil painting (business end of hippo etc), has been watching Kate Humble and Bill Oddie on the goggle box ministering to the nation on the private lives of tiny rodents in their nests etc in the fields with respect to the micely conjugals, social lives and general feeding patterns etc etc.

Inspired by the conduct down the burrow of these two enthusiastic naturists, the Mrs has let it be known that 2007 will see the inception at Molerro's Menageries of a bold new venture - **Ealing Hamsterwatch.** This exciting project, which the wife thought up in no time at all, involves the special care round the clock of our miniscule furry brethren around the Borough and constant surveillance of their holes and nests etc from miniature stake-outs crafted from matchboxes and bits of tarpaulin.

The Mrs has decreed that we must approach local businesses asking if they can agree to sponsor the project. If you're a lucky one out of the hat you will go forward to a draw for a lifetime's supply of hamsters, gerbils or rats, which can be supplied in one go at Christmas, or in a constant sequence right through the year, every year.

Just tick the box below if you don't want publicity should you win the Great Ealing Hamster Draw.

Look forward to hearing soon. We're hoping for strong support from the local constabulary who could well be interested.

Best wishes

Yours sincerely

RM Molerro (Mr)

☐ I do not want to be famous with TVs etc if I win the Massive Hamster Draw (Ealing).

Park View Road
Ealing
London W5

5 December 2006

The Chief Executive
Kays Lifestyle magazine
Royal Avenue
Widnes WA88 1TB

Dear Sir

I am Mr Morello, an Italian gent. I am married to Rosetta Morello (Mrs).

Could you assist with a small item? The wife has a slight problem with her drawers falling down all the time. It's so embarrassing for everyone – Desmond, Kenton and Neville and me. Delia takes it particularly badly and naturally in her state tends to get quite upset.

And the slippage and collapse is always at just the wrong time – they only drop at the supermarket checkout, or when helping out the cubs and brownies as Mother Owl at the Harvest Festival. **The kiddies get quite scared when the drawers start sliding as they're so massive, leading to a general abandonment of the outsize veg etc.**

Do you have any extra strong elastic, or say braces for holding up knickers eg to sling over the shoulders and tie up in a sailor's reversible rolling hitch knot round the back?

Hoping to hear very soon. The "Holy Moses" Interfaith Carol Service is looming on the 16th and no-one wants a repeat of last year's underwear incident which caused serious ramifilications what with Bishop Burgess having to urgently relocate all the pixies to the back of the church, and feeling quite giddy, with Miss Tugg taking over as Senior Choirmistress for a rather faltering **"And Did Those Feet in Ancient Times"**, while the Mrs reassembled her corsetage and bloomers in the outer vestibule.

Please reply to me, not the wife.

Thanking you,

Yours sincerely

RM Morello (Mr)

kays
lifestyle
London Road, Preston, PR1 4BR

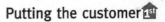

26 January 2007
Reference Number:

Mr R Morello
Park View Road
Ealing
London
W5 2LF

Dear Mr Morello

Thank you for your reply to our letter about assistance your wife requires.

Unfortunately we do not stock strong elastic or braces for holding up underwear.

I am sorry for your wife's embarrassment and trust she will be able to purchase the items locally.

I trust this concludes the matter.

Yours sincerely

Irene Dixon
CUSTOMER SUPPORT

A member of
Littlewoods
Shop Direct Group
The UK's biggest shop @ home group

Littlewoods Shop Direct Home Shopping Limited
Registered in England number 04663281
Registered Office 1st Floor Skyways House
Speke Road Speke Liverpool L70 1AB
VAT Number 163 7696 28

LWSD/0048 10/06

MORELLO'S MENAGERIES

Park View Road
Ealing
London W5
19 December 2006

The Top Magistrate
The Magistrates Association
28 Fitzroy Square
London W1P 6DD

Dear Sir or Madame

Hello. I am Mr Morello. Could I mention something with the possibility of some advisories?

Last Wednesday morning me and the Mrs took Desmond (the lame emu) down to Jeff Snippett, the local vet, to have his claws redacted following a slight punch up with Norris, the fire-dragon, concerning a Weetabix left over after breakfast.

The wife (Rosetta) dropped us off out the back of the Bedford Rascal. Desmond legged it round to Mr Snippett's. I thought I'd pop in the Old Library to check out some literatures.

No sooner did I get in but some bloke festooned in a wig yelled "Hoodies.... stand up!" A load of lads like our Tosti (17) sprung up, with a bouncer-bloke beside them (with hairy arms).

"Got any books in on emus etc?" I yelled to the wigg-bloke.

"Shut it" he cried, "What do you think this is, a library? That's next door! This is the magistrables courts!"

"Hoodies" he continued. "You're all guilty of wearing hoods in the shops, and I sentence you to 10 hours community services -- each. <u>Without</u> your hoods on. Now get lost, and don't hang around the car park. And another thing. Take that ostrich with you."

With that, someone suddenly yelled "Court rise!", and everyone leapt up. By now I noticed Desmond was in the back of the courtroom, with the Mrs. Des was being led out by the bouncer.

Anyway, now every time the wife comes in the lounge, or staggers in from the kitchen with the Brussels etc for dinner she yells "Court rise" or "Hoodies, stand!" Everyone leaps up, including any beasts that happen to be lying around the room.

What is a hoodie anyway, and how come they've copped it when the bloke in the wigg got away with it etc?
All the best. Hoping to hear soon. Apologies for being Italian etc,

RM Morello (Mr)

MAGISTRATES
A S S O C I A T I O N

28 Fitzroy Square
London W1T 6DD

14 May 2007

Mr RM Morello
Park View Road
Ealing
London
W5 2JF

Dear Mr Morello

Thank you for your letter of 5 May 2007.

I can find no record of our having received an earlier letter from you but, now that I have a copy, I am afraid that I still cannot really be of much help to you. The Magistrates' Association is a membership organisation for volunteer magistrates, funded by subscription. We are not a government department or part of the magistrates' courts service so are unable to deal with individual incidents.

I am sorry that I cannot be of more assistance.

Yours sincerely

Sally Dickinson
Chief Executive

END OF CORRESPONDENCE

Park View Road
Ealing
London W5

10 January 2007

The Chief Executive
Fred Olsen Cruises
Fred Olsen House
White House Road
Ipswich IP1 5LL

Dear Sir

I am Mrs Morello. I'm planning a cruise on your top liner shortly, making up a party of me, Stan Bamford and Betty (his wife). And possibly Derek Hogsworth from the garage. And Mr Morello's coming too. We decided on Fred Olsen as definitely the top line for packet steamers etc in the western hemisphere. This followed an unpleasant incident with a rival steamship last summer involving some unusual language – Jeff Tindall, who'd arrived at the cruise half an hour late for the off, made the mistake of asking the Chief Purser where he should hide his valuables. He was in some discomfort for about 10 days.

Anyway we've studied the brochures quite closely and have our itinerarary sorted, and have read all the Qs and As which are quite helpful. Only there's a few things we're still not sure about:

1 Could I bring my own lifeboat? Obviously we hope not to sink but it could be a useful precaution. But anyway the other reason is that I do **not** wish to be left in a confined space (like a lifeboat) with Stan who sweats heavily, and has halitosis of the mouth and feet, so is it permissible for us to be placed the other side of the vessel from him(whether or not we're sinking)? There could be some unpleasant repercussions downwind if he's playing quoits on deck with respect to excessive heat on board.

2 We thought the itinerary for the Med trip was nice but can we stop at Tenerife as well as we'd like to pop in on the Domingos who were so helpful that time with the flip flops at La Tapas back in summer '03.

3 We'd like to bring Kenton and Delia with us who maybe the Captain could oversee if not too busy at the bridgehead? Kenton in particular, whose never set foot off dry land, would love a go at the steering wheel.

Hoping to hear soon.

Yours sincerely

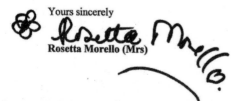

Rosetta Morello (Mrs)

☒ Fred. Olsen Cruise Lines

Direct Tel: 01473 292200
Direct Fax: 01473 292212

Our ref: MR/zjp

14th February 2007

Mrs R Molerro
Park View Road
Ealing
London
W5

Dear Mrs Molerro

I am writing in the hope of explaining a little bit about cruising.

Firstly can I say that we would welcome you and your friends on board one of our vessels as you all seem to be good fun!

In answer to your specific questions:

1 – Unfortunately it will not be possible for you to bring your own lifeboat unless it is a blow up variety with the ducks head at the front. I would suggest that you ask Stan to see a doctor prior to travelling as some of our other passengers may be inconvenienced by his standard of personal hygiene.

2 – If you have any requests about improving our itinerary as we go along please speak with the Captain as I am sure that he will accommodation you if possible. For your Mediterranean cruise I could also suggest that we berth at Milan as I understand the Opera House is well worth a visit.

3- I am sure that we would welcome Kenton and Delia on board, but cannot confirm that the Captain could give them his full attention as he spends much of his time whipping the slaves and trying to catch weevils.

I hope that this answers your queries.

Thank you in anticipation

Yours sincerely

Mike Rodwell
Managing Director
Fred. Olsen Cruise Lines Ltd

END OF CORRESPONDENCE

Fred. Olsen Cruise Lines, Fred. Olsen House, White House Road, Ipswich, Suffolk IP1 5LL
Tel: 01473 292200 Fax: 01473 292201 www.fredolsencruises.co.uk
Registered No. 2672435 Kings Scholars House, 230 Vauxhall Bridge Road, London SW1V 1AU VAT No. GB 676693769

93

WEST LONDON OVATES AND BARDS

Park View Road
Ealing
London W5

11 January 2007

The General Manager
Glasgow Rangers FC
Ibrox Stadium
150 Edmiston Drive
Glasgow G51 2XD

Dear Sir

I am writing to enquire if we may hire the Stadium for a colossal meeting of druids, ovates and some bards, probably as we approach the Spring Equinox. We had in mind Friday 9 March from 5.30 pm till about 11.15pm. This will tie in nicely with later preparations for Beltane, when we receive the guidance of the tribe and its mythos.

Could we each hold a candle? We would also like to bring about 90 sheeps and goats, and erect an enormous TV screen.

There will be some general worship of the Om, and Cliff Richard will be leading a sing song.

Would you tell us how much? Will it be more with Cliff there, due to the singing?

All the best

Yours sincerely

Rosetta Morello (Mrs)
Secretary-General

THE
RANGERS
FOOTBALL CLUB plc
Founded 1873

18 January 2007

Mrs Rosetta Morello
Park View Road
Ealing
London
W5

Dear Mrs Morello

Thank you for your recent letter.

I was very intrigued to learn of the proposed *'colossal meeting of druids, ovates and some bards'* and was delighted to note that you are considering holding this event at Ibrox Stadium.

I can confirm that we would have no objection to each attendee holding a candle (on the basis that it remained unlit at all times) and that we would welcome your plan to bring along *'90 sheeps and goats'* - I have no doubt that their sacrifice will prove to be a most charming spectacle.

I note that during the *'general worship of the Om'* you intend proceedings to be led by one 'Cliff Richard' and I regret that this does present a major stumbling block. Mr Richard, quite aside from his remarkable talents in the field of singer-song writing and wine-making, is a well established football hooligan and rogue of the worst sort. He and various members of his 'firm' the so-called 'Shadows' are subject to banning orders which prevent their attendance at football stadia throughout the country

Whilst we will be unable to accept your booking as it currently stands, should you decide to proceed without the services of Mr Richard we would of course be delighted to welcome you. A sum of £25,000,000.00 would secure the stadium for the evening in question subject to various stipulations being met, including your agreement that only limited human sacrifice will take place and an assurance that any goats permitted to survive would be prevented from eating the grass.

I look forward to receipt of the £25,000,000.00 to confirm your booking.

Yours sincerely

WILLIAM MACLEOD

TELEPHONE: Customer Services 0870 600 1972   Tickets 0870 600 1993   Hospitality 0870 600 1964   Commercial 0870 600 1899   Retail/Mail Order 0870 599 1997
FACSIMILE: 0870 600 1978   WEBSITE: www.rangers.co.uk
REGISTERED OFFICE: IBROX STADIUM   150 EDMISTON DRIVE   GLASGOW G51 2XD   Registered in Scotland No. 4276

WEST LONDON OVATES AND BARDS

Park View Road
Ealing
London W5

20 January 2007

William Macleod Esq
Glasgow Rangers FC
Ibrox Stadium
150 Edmiston Drive
Glasgow G51 2XD

Dear Mr Macleod

Many thanks for your letter of 18th inst, addressed to the wife, as the Grand Druid for the West London area.

The Mrs is also standing for Resident High Priestess for the Ealing, Northolt and Ruislip coven this summer in a two man play-off against Bunty Bagshawe, which promises to be quite a spectacle. In fact it's quite a gruj match between two ancient foes after all that business at the Ealing Bowls Club last March with Dot Partridge and Desmond the emu. So the Mrs reckons we've got to get the celebrity Om evening spot on to keep up her chances for the Priestess slot.

Thanks for the go-ahead on the human sacrifice. This has cheered the wife up no end as all the other stadiums we tried would only allow it we met a load of health and safety conditions.

You'll be relieved to hear we've made arrangements to bin Cliff for the evening in favour of Lionel Blair, and we'll follow on with the slaughter of the celebrities pageant after the singing. We're hoping Dale Winton and Ann Widdecombe will both be putting in an appearance at some point.

Could you supply grapple bags for the druids who can get rather peckish etc and then get a bit excitable, especially during the Om. The wife reckons carrot slices and a McFlurry should keep them quiet till the main feature. And a Snickers bar, which could be battered and deep fried in sump oil as a nod to local cuisine possibly?

The price is no problem, in fact quite modest compared to the Bernabeu quote (£100m). The cheque's in the post and might arrive about the day after the event. It's drawn on the West London Druids Massacre Account No 1 so there shouldn't be any problem.

See you on the 9th March.

Yours sincerely

RM Morello (Mr)
Administrative Assistant (Events)

PS: The Chief Druid says hi!

PPS: have you got any enormous cooking pots?

END OF CORRESPONDENCE

MOLERRO'S MENAGERIES

Park View Road
Ealing
London W5

8 Septembre 2007

Mr Simon Cowell
Syco TV
Bedford House
69-79 Fulham High Street
London SW6 3JW

Dear Mr Cowell

Mrs Molerro and I have always avidly watched *The X Factor* and are great admirers of the show and its antics. So much so that this summer the Mrs (Rosetta) has started an animal version for the creatures in our menageries, and we're hoping to go live soon with **The Z Factor!** , (which is a Zoo version of the human one).

The idea's a bit similar in that all the beasts in the cages are allowed to put themselves forward for audition before a carefully selected panel of judges where they sing, dance and howl and then we get to have a go at them. Some of the animales get quite excited in the warm ups and turn up with half the flock or nest. There's a gerbil whose convinced he's got the Z Factor, and a little group of 3 lady hamsters in a girl band who have tiny harmonised voices.

There's also a capybara and a marmoset who sing Country 'n' Western together but who're useless.

We've had a bit of trouble with a hyena who couldn't sing for toffees. It was awful! The wife only went and told him to get lost and don't come back. He skulked off but then came back with a load of mates and started snarling at the judges and causing trouble with the competitors. Also his mum was in tears.

We should be opening the competition to all the local fauna(pets __and__ wildlife) quite soon so hoping it's all ok etc with the name. Apparently Rolf Harris and Trevor McDonald are quite interested in being judges. And Cilla Black, probably.

Hoping to hear soon.

Yours sincerely

R. Molerro

R Molerro (Mr)

Any chance you could do the opening?

Park View Road
Ealing
London W5

11 January 2007

Head of the Toy Department
Woolworths
Woolworth House
242-246 Marylebone Road
London NW1 6JL

Dear Sir or Madam

We all love your toys in our family and hope you can give some advice.

Here's some of the presents we got for Christmas this year that we definitely don't want:

Tracey Island playset
Dr Who Cyberman mask (for myself)
Pogo stick (boxed)
Tower of Doom
2 car jacks
a small hat and jerkin combo for the hound, Jet (slightly bitten)
the late aunt's specs (Gregorys)
a scratch post for the jaguar
some electric tinsel (12 yards)
a snail run
a couple of terrapins

Can we change any of them with you, and can you suggest something better? We're interested in goats, dangerous sports, travel ,sheep, making monies (gringos). And hamsters. Hoping to hear soon.

Mrs Schneider at No. 28 said we could change them with you.

Yours sincerely

Rosetta Morello (Mrs)

WOOLWORTHS

Rosetta Morello
53a Park View Road
Ealing London W5

WOOLWORTHS plc
Woolworth House
242/246 Marylebone Road
London
NW1 6JL

Telephone: 020-7706 5815
Facsimile: 020-7479 5199

Dear Mrs Morello,

Friday, 19 January 2007

RE: Unwanted Christmas presents

Thank you for your letter dated 11 January 2007. I am sorry to hear that you received some unwanted presents for Christmas.

Unfortunately, we can only exchange them if they were purchased from Woolworths.

However, we can recommend some alternatives that match your interests.

Goats –
Goat by LL Cool J (CD) – £8.99
Any CD by The Mountain Goats
The Three Billy Goats Gruff Fairy Tale Craft Kit – £14.99

Dangerous sports –
Boxing punchbag and gloves – £9.99
Large Oval Concerto Pool – £4,999.99 (you can practice white water rafting)
WWE figurines – £5.99 each

Travel –
Any trip from www.woolworths.co.uk/travel
(Is this the way to) Amarillo by Tony Christie (digital download) – 59p
Digital Tyre Pressure Guage - £5 (get the right tyre pressure every trip)

Sheep –
Hot Water Bottle Wooly – £10 (the sheep from our ads!)
Key Ring Wooly – £1.99 (all the money goes to charity!)
Chad Valley Tractor and Sheep Trailer – £5.99

Hamsters –
Hamster Jam CD by the Hamsters – £8.99
Digital Pet Hamster – £9.99
Richard Hammond's Car Confidential book - £8.79 (he's known as The Hamster)

Making Monies –
Digital Coin Sorter – £29.99 (count as you go)
Football Skills (book) – £3.29 (footballers earn a lot of money)
Security Waist Wallet – £3.99 (combine with your interest in travel)

Woolworths has 821 high street stores and you can find all these products at www.woolworths.co.uk.

Yours sincerely,

Daniel Himsworth
Woolworths plc

END OF CORRESPONDENCE

Registered & Head Office: Woolworth House 242/246 Marylebone Road London NW1 6JL Registered in England [No 104206]

MORELLO'S MENAGERIES

Park View Road
Ealing
London W5

9 February 2007

Lord Dafyd Elis-Thomas AM
Ty Glyndwr
Heol Glyndwr
Dolgellau
Wales LL40 1BD

Dear Lord Elis-Thomas

Mrs Morello and I have long been admirers of your political opinions and your career. Could we ask your assistance on a point?

Me and the wife's cousins from Sardinia were recently traversing the principality of Wales on a small holiday and really looking forward to it (we were heading for Ireland).

The wife was also with us. She points out that we were very disappointed that there are so few sheeps left in Wales compared to the old days. Almost every loch and burn we drove round presented another unwelcome surprise – no sheeps on the other side of it!

When me and the Mrs were last in the area in 1974 (we inadvertently strayed into Wales by mistake when getting lost in the Sprite on the way up to the Zieglers' 25th in Preston) such beasts were knee deep in the Valleys, and were much appreciated by country folk for their humour, versatility and sense of fun. We also noted that the few sheeps we did see as we spluttered around were surprisingly small, and seemed rather dejected and lacking in confidence. They all ran away when we waved a huge stick at them and Mrs Morello playfully shouted *"Moooo!"*

What exactly is going on here man? Do the sheeps all live indoors? Are they hiding in the National Assembly? What's become of the National Beast of this once proud Land of Dylan Thomas, Owen Glyndwr and Catherine Zeta Jones-Douglas? <u>I noticed there wasn't one mention of a single sheep on the National Assembly's website.</u>

Let's start celebrating this woolly totem once again.

Hoping to hear soon. Thanks for your help.

Yours sincerely

RM Morello (Mr)

Dafydd Elis-Thomas AC/AM

Ffôn/Tel: 01341 422 661
Ffacs/Fax: 01341 423 990
E-bost/E-mail:
dafydd.elis-thomas@wales.gov.uk

Swyddfa'r Etholaeth
Ty Glyndwr
Heol Glyndwr
Dolgellau
Gwynedd
LI40 1BD

Cynulliad   National
Cenedlaethol Assembly for
Cymru   Wales

Mr R. M Morello
53a Park View Road
EALING
London
W5

Mr Morello

Thank you for your recent letters and I apologise for the delay in responding.

I have raised your concerns with the Wales Government's Minister for Agriculture.

I will contact you again as soon as I have received the Minister's response.

Yours sincerely

Dafydd Elis-Thomas
AM DWYFOR MEIRIONNYDD
" 16|07

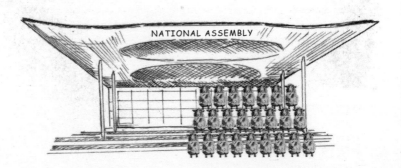

NATIONAL ASSEMBLY

Park View Road
Ealing
London W5

25 May 2007

The Senior Adviser
Visit Wales
Welsh Assembly Government
Brunel House
2 Fitzalan Road
Cardiff CF24 0UY

Dear Sir or Madam

I am writing on behalf of a large group of oriental persons who will be visiting the Principality of Wales in the summer for a cultural trip. I wanted to ask some questions that Mrs Morello and I are convinced will be of interest to the Japanese visitors when they descend on your shores:

1 roughly how many castles do you estimate inhabit Wales presently? (Mrs Morello thought about 6000 or so so hopefully it's about that).

2 do you still have lots of sheep in the area? Roughly how many? When we were driving through the area in the Sprite back in the 1970s there seemed to be far less of this once woolly totem than had appeared in the movies. They also seemed quite small and nervous whereas once such beasts were secreted on every loch and burn the whole length of Wales, from Stonehenge to Fishbourne.

3 Will it be possible for the Jap. folks to communicatate with the Welsh without misapprehensions? For example do many Welsh speak Japanese or will our visitors have to learn Welsh or a similar dialect in order to find basic food and shelter?

4 Could you write out for us in the Welsh dialect **" We are Japs, we come in peace and harmony from Japan. Please accept this gift of shark meat. Can you now lead us to a traditional Indian takeaway".**

We are most grateful for your help. Looking forward to hearing soon.

Best wishes

From
R Morello (Mr)

Wales View

Gyda chyfarchion
With compliments

Visit Wales
Croeso Cymru

Y. Mr Mulley /

END OF CORRESPONDENCE

Llywodraeth Cynulliad Cymru,
Yr Adran Menter, Arloesi a Rhwydweithiau, Tŷ Brunel,
2 Ffordd Fitzalan, Caerdydd CF24 0UY

Welsh Assembly Government,
Department for Enterprise, Innovation & Networks,
Brunel House, 2 Fitzalan Road, Cardiff CF24 0UY

Ffôn/Telephone
Ffacs/Facsimile
E-bost/Email
www.visitwales.com

Llywodraeth Cynulliad Cymru
Welsh Assembly Government

Issue 01__2007

Pembrokeshire unearthed with Tony Robinson
Caroline Stacey on the slow food trail
Rob Ryan in the Brecon Beacons
Roger Thomas rides the Snowdon Sherpa
Ian Woosnam's golfing favourites

Plus travel and holiday information
Plus travel and holiday information

Wales
Cymru

Park View Road
Ealing
London W5

28 July 2007

The Rt Rev John Pritchard
The Bishop of Oxford
Christ Church Cathedral
St Aldate's
OXFORD

Dear Bishop Oxford

I am Mr Molerro. I am also married to Mrs Molerro. The wife is a staunch adherent of
the C of E and a strong advocate of almost anything that enters her head.

We're shortly moving into the area (with the kids) and the Mrs has set her heart on
founding a new parish. She's looking around for suitable premises and seems to wonder
if you could purvey a spare building possibly? Meanwhile she's conducted a few
interviews and reckons she's sorted the line up for the parish officers to look like this:

The Reverend Basil Scrimshaw DD MA (vicar and team leader)

Godfrey Cheeseman (curate and general purposes/ sweeper)

Major General Sir Percival Henman-Hill (retd.) (roof lead and lightning conductor)

Audrey Potsdam MBE WRVS (Ms) (jam)

Beryl Trotfoot (worship co-ordinator)

Cedric Partridge (*Holy Moses!* hymn books)

Sister Philomena Dunphy (floral displays)

Brian Sidgwick (carpentry)

Bunty Hinchcliffe (teas and scones)

Senora Carmen Fondamenta de las Obrigados (cushions) – *and her cousin…*

Senor Severiano Fondamento Huevo de los Nacarenas (light bulbs)

Doris Fudge (church mice)

I find the Mrs' thinking on this matter somewhat impenetrable but experience dictates
that she can be pretty tricky to shift. If you can do any better, eg by setting her right with
a letter, this would be much appreciated.

Hoping to hear soon. Don't mention I wrote in.

Yours sincerely

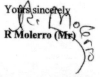

R Molerro (Mr)

THE DIOCESE OF OXFORD

ARCHDEACONRIES OF BERKSHIRE . BUCKINGHAM . OXFORDSHIRE

FROM THE BISHOP OF OXFORD
The Rt Reverend John Pritchard

Mr R Molerro
Park View Road
EALING
LONDON W5

9 August 2007

\\dbf.local\data\Users\christine\Documents\AUGUST\RMMIS.doc

Dear Mr. Molerro,

Thank you for your most interesting letter. Your wife sounds to be a very imaginative person and to have assembled a remarkable line-up of parish officers, many of whom I think I've already met in different parishes with different names. I wonder if she would consider Audrey Heartstop-Frothington (coffee and cream).

As for a spare church building to take over, our plans are to fill them all with joyful worshippers within a generation. I hope you good wife will continue to dream on.

With all good wishes

Yours sincerely

+John

Diocesan Church House, North Hinksey Lane, Oxford OX2 0NB
Tel: Oxford (01865) 208222   Fax: Oxford (01865) 790470
E-mail: bishopoxon@oxford.anglican.org   www.oxford.anglican.org

THE DIOCESE OF OXFORD

BERKSHIRE · BUCKINGHAMSHIRE · OXFORDSHIRE

FROM THE BISHOP OF OXFORD'S PERSONAL ASSISTANT
Christine Lodge

*We assume Don's fudge is no
Church cat   ?*

With Compliments

Diocesan Church House, North Hinksey Lane, Oxford OX2 0NB
Tel: Oxford (01865) 208222   Fax: Oxford (01865) 790470
E-mail: christine.lodge@oxford.anglican.org   www.oxford.anglican.org

MORELLO'S MENAGERIES

Park View Road
Ealing
London W5

11 August 2007

The Rt Rev John Pritchard
The Bishop of Oxford
Diocesan Church House
North Hinksey Lane
Oxford OX2 0NB

Dear Bishop Oxon

Thanks a lot for your epistle of the 9th inst, with a small codicil attached from Christine Lodge which fluttered out and struck Titan the toy poodle on the nose who was barking for about the next 2.5 hours.

I've mentioned your suggestion to the Mrs about the other Audrey. I had to pick a good moment given what I noted this morning: the wife staggering down the stairs, festooned with curlers and a face like thunder, muttering dark incantations in the general direction of our eldest (Tosti,17). The hopeless idle lad, the bane of our lives and even on an industrious day doing a passable imitation of a pot plant, had only gone and left the side gate open last night so that Enoch the goat and several of the pets had slid through and done a runner down the hill, pursued by Marvin the hedgehog.

For Tosti the effort involved in swinging a gate closed on its hinges after carrying through a sack of emu feed broadly corresponds to the labours of Sisyphus. So now we're about 30% down on the beasts' roll call for the menageries' summer season!

Anyhow the Mrs is thinking up a way to bin Audrey P from the new parish committee in favour of your Audrey, who she has in fact met at Mabel Winthrop's summer whist drive at "Ivanhoe" (turn left down the end of North Hinksey Lane, then second right at the Badger and Ferret), and took something of a shine to her having cleared up rather nicely at everyone else's expense. Anyway I'll keep you posted.

As to the codicil, Miss Fudge is not the church cat. She is in fact a general dogsbody who feels that daily communion with even the tiniest of God's creatures brings us closer to an understanding of the Great Unknown. However it was still a shock to the Mrs when last at the Parish of St Filbert's (now defunct) to spot that, far from despatching the tiny rodents into oblivion, Doris was enthusiastically breeding them in jam jars in the church potting shed. So there could be another Committee slot opening up there.

Looking forward to hearing.

Yours respectfully,

RM. Mre

RM Morello (Mr)

END OF CORRESPONDENCE

Park View Road
Ealing
London W5

5 August 2007

The Director
Birmingham Art Gallery
Chamberlain Square
Birmingham B3 3DH

Dear Sir

Unfortunately the wife's cousins the Buffonis are visiting in force for the summer from Manzana (Sicily) and we're touring up the north and in the Midd-lands of the Ingland.

Mrs B (Massima) is quite keen to acquaint some Inglish art and hopes to see something contemporary. In London we have some spectacles such as a demi-shark creation swimming in formaldyhide which Mrs Morello (Rosetta) states is quite an amazing and unusual spectacle and a near miracle of nature.

Do you have much art being in Birmingham which is quite high up near the north? Anyway do you have anything similar as we believe the Buffonis would like this being from a seafaring background?

Mrs B had an accidental on the way over via Venezia where she caught her heel in the top end of the ramp of the vaparetto and slid all the way down which caused some damages to the bottom.

So now Massima is indisposed a bit from walking on the legs. Anyway Salvatore has created a special velocette walking bed with sticks and things and a hood and wheels that go round. Is it OK if 'e brings the contrapzione into the gallerie laden with Mrs B to inspect any demi-shark you may have and also the works of art?

Looking forward to coming probably about 2.30pm on 16 August (Thursday). Please let us know if there's a problem as there'll be quite a lot of us showing.

Apologies for the Inglish being Italian.

Best wishes

Yours sincerely

R Molerro (Mr)

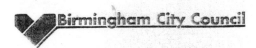**Birmingham City Council**

Mr R Molero
Park View Road
Ealing
London
W5

Friday 10th August 2007

Caro signore Molero,

Sono molto felice che ha deciso di portare sua famiglia a Birmingham.
Il museo e situado nel centro della citta e e uno di molti luoghi da visitare.
Mi dispiace che la signora Buffoni si e fatto male e spero che non soffre
molto.
Siamo aperto dale 10 alle 5 e non si paga per entrare.
Al momento, abbiamo una mostra contenporanea che si chiama
"How to improve the world" dal British Arts Council e un'altra " Paula
Rego, Graven images". Mi dispiace pero non abbiamo un mezzo squalo.
Siamo famosi per nostra collezione di quadri del 18 secolo.
Si puo vedere parte della nostra collezione a www.bmag.org.uk
Un problemo possible e che per entrare nel museo, tutti devonno utilizzare
le scale o un'ascensore che sara puodarsi troppo piccolo per la
contrapzione fatta per la signora.

Se vuole telefonarmi, 0121 464 4335, possiamo parlare delle misure per
essere siguro che lei puo utilizarlo.
Ho aggiunto qualche volantini per aiutarlo e spero di verdervi a
Birmingham.

Pat Ferrins

Pat Ferrins
Assistant Visitors Services Manager

awarded for excellence

Directorate of Children, Young People & Families

Birmingham Museums & Art Gallery
Chamberlain Square
Birmingham
B3 3DH

Telephone: 0121-303-2834
Facsimile: 0121-303-1394

Park View Road
Ealing
London W5

13 August 2007

Ms Pat Ferrins
Assistant Visitors Services Manager
Birmingham Art Gallery
Chamberlain Square
Birmingham B3 3DH

Dear Ms Ferrins

My name is Robin Dovecote. I am the Molerros' lodger. I live in their attic (I am a poet and am quite sensitive to noise so I just keep to myself up here).

The Molerros have gone on a tour of England with Mrs Molerro's relatives the Buffonis who are over from Sicily for a look around the place and they've left me in charge of *Casa Molerro* and the menageries in the back garden! It was quite frightening at first as I was once set upon by a couple of the stoats and Titan joined in.

Every morning after feeding the goats and emus I quietly lead Enoch and Desmond down to Tresco's for some foodstuffs and bedding (I just eat a little gruel and scraps of bread being quite poetical) then we go to Pitshanger Park where we have a bit of a walk, and I do a reading. Kenton has been joining us recently as he's quite interested in olde-tyme ballads and romances which I'm writing at the moment and definitely has artistic tendencies.

Anyway when we've all trailed back home with the shopping I have a lie down in my garret to recover myself then we open the post together as Mrs Molerro told me to do. Kenton does the parcels and I do the rest.

This morning I opened your letter dated Friday 10 August. I noticed this was from Birmingham Art Gallery but full of foreign words, possibly Grecian or Latin. I was wondering if it was a love letter to Mr Molerro from when he visited Birmingham that time to deliver a load of gerbils to *"Rodents R Us"* down the Hagley Road and maybe he met someone romantically (and forgot to tell Mrs Molerro about it). I got rather emotional reading it, and started feeling quite giddy.

Could you perchance do a translation into English (or early Anglo-Saxon if you prefer as I do all my ballads in that)? Then if I can get Mrs M off the phone when she next rings in to check up I can read it out to Mr Molerro rather quietly and see if perhaps he would commission me to pen an impassioned reply from him, possibly in the form of a sonnet. Or even a ballad. When I've got over my summer chill.

Hoping to hear soon.

Yours sincerely

Robin Dovecote

Robin Dovecote (poet)

END OF CORRESPONDENCE

MOLERRO'S MENAGERIES

Park View Road
Ealing
London W5
March 10th, 2008

Mrs Clare Coxall
South View
Church Road
Burstow
Surrey RH6 9RG

Dear Mrs Coxall

Mr Molerro and I run a little menageries here in West London having recently moved from Italia.

We have both been watching the Cruft's (dogshow) transfixed. We wanted to write to say what a marvellous job you did in the competition and to congratulate you on Best in Show. We felt you performed with great elegance, poise and confidence.

We were pleased to note that you mentioned to Clare Balding that appearing at Cruft's helps you with your breeding. You certainly seemed to thoroughly enjoy yourself.

We are holding a show of emus and ostriches for the West London and Middlesex area on **Sunday May 4th** – here in Ealing. There will be a widespread gathering of flightless avians arriving from all over the area in trailers, flatbacks and Transits. You may even spot a cassowary and even a rhea or miniature kiwi or two!

Would you be able to attend as our guest celebrity to judge the best bird of the lot? It would be a great honour and thrill if you might do so. Kick off's 2pm which will have given the creatures time to calm down a bit after the journey and to stretch their legs and spend a penny in the back garden.

Hoping to hear soon.

Thanking you,

Yours sincerely

Rosetta Molerro (Mrs)

TiOPEPi POODLES

1, Lopen Head
South Petherton
Somerset
TA13 5JH

March 25th 2008

Mrs Rosetta Molero,
Park View Road
Ealing
London W5

Dear Mrs Molero,

Thank you so much for your letter of the 10th. I am delighted that you gained so much pleasure from watching me judge Best in Show at Crufts. People have been so kind about my performance, which brought to a head the many years of hard work and dedication that I have given to my sport. Truly this was an unforgettable climax.

I was very interested to learn that you are holding a show of emus and ostriches for the West London and Middlesex area on Sunday May 4th in Ealing. If you have read some of the many pre-Crufts interviews that the press have conducted with me, you will be aware that wildlife photography is another of my passions, and with my knowledge of livestock and construction I would look forward to judging for you.

My problem is that I have a prior engagement that morning, however a friend of mine who owns his own helicopter has kindly agreed to fly me in to Ealing in time for judging and fly me out again, subject to the proximity of the nearest helipad.

Perhaps you could let me have details of available facilities as soon as possible,

Yours sincerely,

Clare Coxall (Mrs.)

MOLERRO'S MENAGERIES

Park View Road
Ealing
London W5

March 27th, 2008

Mrs Clare Coxall
Senior Judge (Emus and Ostriches)
Tiopepi Poodles
1 Lopen Head
South Petherton
Somerset TA13 5JH

Dear Mrs Coxall

Many thanks for your lettre of March 25rd regarding your success re best in Show at Cruft's.

We're very thrilled you can stand in judgment over the emus etc. In fact all the beasts around the menageries got quite excited when your missive arrived, and there was a colossal din in the tamarinds' cages overnight when the word got out!

I don't think we've ever had a helichopter in Ealing before. Could you land in the allotments behind the back garden? We could flatten out the turnip beds. The more nervous competitors like the cassowaries could get a bit scared and think some massive hawk had arrived. So we're going to fit them up with little hoods and some tiny ear plugs. Apparently they quite like a bit of sensory deprivation about once a week.

By the by Molerro's operates a **strictly No Dogs policy,** and especially No Poodles, (though we do have a poodle-type thing made out of ~~tioparry tiopersio~~ the hedge in the front garden). It started out as a llama. The policy's cos flightless birds and fluffy poodles just don't go together: park a poodle near a penguin and you've got a bloodbath on your hands. Hence the demise of the mighty Dodo.

So could you leave any mutts in the chopter whilst adjudicating?

Hoping to hear soon.

Rolf Harrison the celebrity is definitely coming probably.

Can we have a go in the chopter before it flies off?

All the best,

Yours sincerely

Rosetta Molerro
Rosetta Molerro (Mrs)

END OF CORRESPONDENCE

Park View Road
Ealing
London W5

5 August 2007

Sir Nicholas Serota
Director
The Tate Gallery
Millbank
London SW1P 4RG

Dear Sir-ota

The Mrs is very keen to inspect the demi-shark creation swimming in formaldyhide at your gallery which we believe is quite an amazing and unusual spectacle and a near miracle of nature.

Could you confirm when the creature will be available for scrutiny please?

Unfortunately the wife's cousins the Buffonis are visiting in force for the summer from Manzana (Sicily) – and staying in the outquarters down the end of the garden.

Mrs B (Massima) had an accidental on the way over via Venezia where she caught her heel in the top end of the ramp of the vaporetto and slid all the way down which caused some damages to the bottom.

Massima is now indisposed a bit from walking on the legs. Anyway Salvatore has created a special velocette walking bed with sticks and things and a hood and wheels that go round. Is it OK if 'e brings this contrapzione (as 'e calls it) into the gallerie laden with Mrs B to inspect the demi-shark and also the works of art?

Looking forward to coming probably about 2.30pm on 16 August (Thursday). Please let us know if there's a problem as there'll be quite a lot of us showing.

Apologies for the Inglis being Italian.

Yours sincerely

RM Morello (Mr)

PS: Didn't there used to be a half a cow on display also swimming in some broth which was replaced possibly after a fight with the shark?

114

Millbank
London SW1P 4RG

call
+44 (0) 20 7887 8000
fax
+44 (0) 20 7887 8007

visit
www.tate.org.uk

TG4.2

14 August 2007

R Molerro Esq
Park View Road
Ealing
London
W5 2JF

Dear Mr Molerro

Thank you for your letter to Sir Nicholas Serota of 5 August regarding your interest in visiting Tate to see works by Damien Hirst.

The shark subject works to which I believe you are referring are Hirst's *The Physical Impossibility of Death in the Mind of Someone Living*, 1991, and *Death Explained*, 2007. Neither of these is in fact owned by Tate, nor are they currently on display in our galleries. Both works have, however, been exhibited recently, the former in *Re-Object* at the Bregenz Kunsthaus (18 February - 13 May 2007), and the latter in *Beyond Belief* at White Cube, Mason's Yard (3 June - 7 July 2007).

If you are interested in Damien Hirst's works may I suggest that you contact White Cube, the gallery which represents the artist, for further information: www.whitecube.com, tel. 020 7930 5373.

Yours sincerely

Administrative Assistant
Director's Office

Park View Road
Ealing
London W5

19 August 2007

Administrative Assistant – Director's Office
The Tate Gallery
Millbank
London SW1P 4RG

Dear Ma'am

Many thanks for your lettre of Augusto 14th with references to the demi-shark belonging to Damian Hurst.

We had no idea the shark-creature was so old as 1991 and also that there is a possible **second** shark from this year which is amazing.

Here at *Molerro's* we run a variety of services and Mrs Molerro always has a hatful of ideas. She's recently taken up the dark arts of painting and has hi hopes of an exhibitionism at the Tate or similar. She's read your lettre and asserts that she's got a few titles in mind for some artworks. Here goes:

The unbearable lightness of being a stoat.

Curlers, dishmop and a bucket (Still life No 12);

The loneliness of the long-distance runner bean.

The Laughing Cavalierro (with beard)

Shark with goat;

The oeuvres have not yet been produced but the Mrs says allow about 3 days for each, and a week should do it for the shark/goat confection.

Could Sir Nicholas or yourself confirm you can hang these around Christmas time then the Mrs will get on with it. They're all oil on canvas but the last is water colore . As soon as we hear back she'll start knocking them out.

Cash on delivery and I can drop them round to exhibitate. Unless maybe Sir Nicholas is passing by and has room in the bute.

Apologies for the Inlis which is better than Mrs Molerro's.

Yours sincerely

RM Molerro (Signore)

116

MOLERRO'S BUSINESS ICONS

Park View Road
Ealing
London W5

March 23rd 2008

Rt Hon Lord Heseltine of Thenford CH
Thenford House
Thenford
Northamptonshire

Dear Lord

We met briefly last month at Coutts Bank's headquarters.

I would like to enquire whether, as a well-known celebrity, you would consent to your name going forward to the next round of the **"British Business Icons"** competition?

This is a prestigious annual event open only to those deemed by a top panel of professional experts to have cleared the bar of excellence for attainment and enterprise in business and industry in modern Britain.

Entry is open to candidates both dead and alive. May we recommend you clearly mark your Entry Form "Living". Success in either category leads to eligibility for accession to the highly prestigious *Molerro's Academy of Stars.* Many, like yourself My Lord, have already bailed out and departed the field of battle. Others are struggling on against the odds, still hoping for the success and accession to The Academy which will never come their way.

Marks will be awarded by the panel for innovation, endeavour, business ethics and durability.

In the next round you will be up against some stiff competition: Sir Alan Sugar, Sir Alex Ferguson and several TV dragons. And Rolf Harris.

At the Grand Final a speech will be given by a celebrity star, possibly Mrs Molerro herself (me) – hailed as a leading figure in her chosen sector (menageries), on *"Cashing in Your Chips and Filling Your Boots – 12 Tips on making a shedload in the Modern World".*

Should you feel ready for this exciting challenge please just drop us a line – It really is as simple as that! You will then receive an information pack with a step-by-step guide on what to do next. There is no entry fee.

Hoping to hear soon.

Yours sincerely

Rosetta Molerro (Mrs)

The Rt Hon the Lord Heseltine, CH

31st March 2008

Mrs Rosetta Molerro
Park View Road
Ealing
London W5

Dear Mrs Molerro

Thank you for your letter of 23rd March regarding "British Business Icons".

I'm afraid I do not wish to take part in this event. I receive many similar requests and simply cannot respond favourably to them all, but I appreciate your thinking of me.

Yours sincerely

The Rt Hon the Lord Heseltine CH

MOLERRO'S BUSINESS ICONS

Park View Road
Ealing
London W5

March 23rd 2008

Rt Hon Lord Heseltine of Thenford CH
Thenford House
Thenford
Northamptonshire

Dear My Lord

Thank you very much for your letter of March 31st ref my **"British Business Icons"** venture.

I can only agree Milord that many of these sorts of initiatives are parlous in their conception or execution, lacking the sparkle and dazzle that the now-famous Molerro brand has come to be renowned for.

I wonder Lord if I may mention that this pageant will also be different from the rest in that it will be held **entirely in the nude.**

I can also add, should this swing the decision, that Baroness Thatcher has **not** been invited.

Hoping to hear soon.

Yours sincerely

Rosetta Molerro (Mrs)

Park View Road
Ealing
London W5

8 Septembre 2007

The Senior Director
The Womens Institute
104 New King's Road
Fulham
London SW6 4LY

Dear Madam

Mrs Morello and I have recently inherited two large adjacent factory premises near Dungeness which we are clearing out so as to re-equip our bakery business.

Meanwhile we have to shift the stock we've found inside. It's quite a combo of gear due to the premises having been used for both a kiddies' toys' business and as an old Army ordnance site.

We're wondering if you know where we might shift the stuff? The Mrs has made up a list:

 Jigsaws
 Teddy bears
 Pressed flowers
 Hand grenades
 Tea cosies
 Anti-aircraft heat-seeking surface to air missiles
 "Death Storm" rocket launchers
 Fluffy posies
 MK47 combat rifles
 Floral cushion covers
 Scented candles
 Cribbage sets
 Tankbuster shells
 Flamethrowers
 Stuffed poodles
 Nuclear bomb shelter

Would any of these be of interest in your branches? Obviously we would take care removing them in controlled conditions: poodles can so easily explode when you least expect.

Looking forward to hearing.

Yours sincerely

RM Morello (Mr)

National Federation
of Women's Institutes

104 New Kings Road
London SW6 4LY

tel: 020 7371 9300
fax: 020 7736 3652
e-mail: hq@nfwi.org.uk
website: www.theWI.org.uk

18th September 2007

R. Molerro, Esq.
Park View Road,
Ealing,
London W5

Dear Mr. Molerro,

Thank you for your letter of 8th September advising us of the items that you have available for disposal.   It was very kind of you to think of the NFWI, but I regret that we will be unable to make use of the items on offer.   I do hope you and Mrs. Molerro manage to dispose of the items in your possession.

Best wishes,

Yours sincerely,

Jana Osborne

Jana Osborne,
General Secretary.

Incorporated in England & Wales as a Company Limited by Guarantee - No. 251 7690. Charity Registration No. 803793. VAT No. 239 4128 57.
Chair: Fay Mansell. Honorary Treasurer: Aleathia Mann. General Secretary: Jana Osborne.
RECYCLED PAPER

Park View Road
Ealing
London W5

January 29th, 2008

Jeremy Paxman Esq
Chief Inquisitor
Newsnight
The BBC
Wood Lane
London W12

Dear Mr Paxman

Mrs Molerro has been reading a bit about your problems with undergarments recently.
I noticed the wife (Rosetta) sitting at the breakfast table yesterday morning festooned
in curlers and a facial mudpack, chuckling at the story in the paper about *"widespread
gusset anxiety",* and your grave concerns about the collapse of modern British
underwear.

The wife suddenly howled like a banshee when she spotted Sir Stuart Rose, chief
honcho at Marks and Spencers, springing to the defence of his shop's corsetage etc.
The Mrs has long been acquatinted with Sir Rose, and knows him to have no need of
socks and pants and the rest, being a well-established nudist over about 50 years or so
down South Ealing way (though latterly somewhat shrivelled around the shanks and
adjoining parts). **So how come he's an expert all of a sudden? the wife enquires.**

Here's hoping the support issues will unravel themselves and hoping to hear soon.
Could you perhaps get through Newsnight in a loincloth, possibly?

Apologies we're Italian.

Yours sincelery

RM Molerro (Signor)

PS: Anyway the Reverend Scrimshaw, who was over for lunch on Boxing Day from
his parish at St Barbara's, Windsor complained of a gusset-comfort issue during the
longer sermons. The Mrs was able to defray the chafing with some llama fur from the
menageries. We weren't sure whether to mention this bit necessarily.

British Broadcasting Corporation Room G680 Television Centre Wood Lane London W12 7RJ

Telephone 020 8624 9800 Fax 020 8743 1102

BBC

Newsnight
bbc.co.uk/newsnight

Signor R M Molerro

Park View Road

Ealing

London W5

11th February 2008

Dear Signor Molerro

Thank you so much for your letter about the Battle for Better Underwear. I was amused to hear your comments about Sir Stuart Rose.

The crusade starts now!

Best wishes

Jeremy Paxman
BBC Newsnight

INVESTOR IN PEOPLE

Park View Road
Ealing
London W5

February 16th, 2008

Jeremy Paxman Esq
Grand Inquisitor and Head of Crusades (underwear)
Newsnight
Room G680 The BBC
Wood Lane
London W12 7RJ

Dear Mr Paxman

Thanks alot for your lettre about underpants and gussets and the rest.

It's so encouraging to know this issue of gents privates etc above everything is in such safe hands at the top of the agenda flagpole.

The Mrs was delighted about the Crusade, stating she has bought a special helmet and sword which she's going to try out at M & S (Ealing Broadway) this morning.

The wife states you can be in charge of the crusade to begin with before she takes over, and meanwhile she'll deal with the Ladies Department. In fact her bloomers are always hitting the deck when least expected eg at the Harvest Festival last Sept., which frightened all the pixies away from the outsize veg and caused Bishop Burgess a slight murmur.

Please could you advise when you are meeting Sir Rose the wife enquires, so she can prepare the implementations.

Hoping to hear soon. Sorry about the Inglis which is better than the Mrs.

Yours sincerely

R Molerro (Mr)

PS: Her bloomers are massive.

British Broadcasting Corporation Room G680 Television Centre Wood Lane London W12 7RJ

Telephone 020 8624 9800 Fax 020 8743 1102

B B C

Newsnight
bbc.co.uk/newsnight

Mr R Molerro
Park View Road
Ealing
London
W5

11th March 2008

Dear Mr Molerro,

I think I'm scared of your wife....

Yours sincerely,

Jeremy Paxman

INVESTOR IN PEOPLE

MOLERRO'S MENAGERIES

Park View Road, Ealing, London W5
8th February 2008

The Senior Partner
Herbert Smith (solicitors)
Exchange House
Primrose Street
London EC2H 2HS

Dear Mr Smith

Last week me and the Mrs, (Rosetta), were travelling up homewards in the Bedford Rascal and trailer from Terry Shrimpton's *"World of Critters"* in Bexhill-on-Sea, laden with a pile of new beasts for the menageries.

Careering around bits of London unfortunately not familiar to her, the wife clipp'd a bollard (concrete), took a couple of wrong turnings and then, lo and behold, we got lost. I got out to soothe the llamas and the muskrat whilst checking the dent on the offside wing, while the Mrs struck out on foot with Enoch and Kenton to seek directions. Then a bit of a deluge started up. So the trio took shelter in a massive barn-type place, which the wife mistook as a bistro – and only went and ordered a cappuccino and Viennese whirls, with milkshakes for the others.

Anyway the gaff turned out to be your place being a load of offices. Whilst relaxing on the sofas, flicking through the mags and brochures whilst the sun remained indoors, Mrs Molerro spotted that you have partners called **Mr Turtle** and **Mr Tortoishell. This seems a good combo, and as a result Mrs Molerro is in a position to advise that we are able to instruct your firm with a new case concerning a collection of dud emus we acquired last summer from an overseas gentleman with a suit on and sunglasses who we encountered at Shepherd's Bush Market and which keep losing their feathers and foliage.**

Talking of muskrats, they're about a foot long (0.3 of a metre), scales on the tail and feet like ducks. They're called musk rats cos they smell of musk, and have massive claws. And a load of whiskers. They live in holes by rivers. They never live up trees, and in Canada they make them into soup and onions. They look a bit like opossums, which they also eat with onions.

Finally they BBQ racoons, and eat squirrels (squirrel cobbler).

Hoping to hear soon. Apologies for being Italain. We'll come round on Tuesday 19th Feb. if that's Ok, about 2.30.

Yours sincerely

R Molerro (Mr)

PS: Mrs Molerro wasn't so pleased about your other partners, called Mr Fox and Mr Peacock, as that could cause problems. Have you got any fish the wife has just enquired? She's just spotted one of them is in fact a Pyke, though we weren't sure whether to mention that as it's not a fish anyway (which is P-I-K-E).

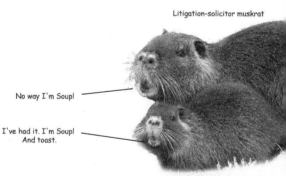

Litigation-solicitor muskrat

No way I'm Soup!

I've had it. I'm Soup!
And toast.

Ordinary-solicitor muskrat

Herbert Smith

Mr R Molerro
Molerro's Menageries
Park View Road
Ealing
London
W5

Herbert Smith LLP
Exchange House
Primrose Street
London EC2A 2HS
T +44 (0)20 7374 8000
F +44 (0)20 7374 0888
DX 28
www.herbertsmith.com

Our ref   2071
Your ref
Date   18 March 2008

Dear Sirs,

We write further to your letter, dated 8 February.

Your letter provides sufficient information to enable us to advise that we would not be able to assist you. This firm deals only with very substantial matters, primarily for commercial clients and we do not consider that it would be cost effective for you to instruct us.

May we suggest that you speak to the Law Society, who might be able to put you in touch with other firms that might be able to assist.

Yours faithfully,

END OF CORRESPONDENCE

MOLERRO'S MENAGERIES

Park View Road
Ealing
London W5

19th March 2008

The Top Director
The Food Standards Agency
Aviation House
125 Kingsway
London WC2B 6NH

Dear Sir or Madam

We run a nice little menageries here in West Ealing, with an emphasis on piggs, hogs, boors, swine and also Mrs Molerro who helps out sometimes.

The beasts are quite big eaters and seem to be consumpting more pigg-food than ever before. Also our kids (Tosti, Amphora and Rizzo) are growing apace so they're leaving less on the sides of the plates than usual.

So now we're looking to find some more mush to shovel into the troughs for the hogg-community waiting anxiously in the pens.

Can you put us in touch with anyone who can provide loads of wet food sludge that would fit the bill? The wife (Rosetta) thought <u>The Association of Swill Users</u> might come into it possibly, but wasn't sure if they dish it out or eat it. Also do you know any big restaurants where maybe the food isn't any good so there's lots of leftovers probably? (maybe Gordon Ramsdens).

Meanwhile could we feed the porkers up on Mrs O'Riordan's turnips and sprouts? (Anyway she's away in Tenerife for two weeks with Maeve and Tommy).

One Friday night we fed the piggs a load of curries that the Patels at No. 32 had chucked out. The wife also gave them some beer we had, in buckets. **After some heavy guzzling all h*ll broke loose, with the heftier male hoggs going a bit mental, shouting the odds and trying to get frisky with the lady-hoggs, then not managing anything and just falling over and going to sleep, snoring heavily and making unusual noises (at both ends).**

Hoping to hear soon.

Yours sincerely

R Molerro (Mr)

From the Correspondence Secretary,
Graham Buckley

Mr R Molerro
Molerro's Menageries
Park View Road
Ealing
London W5

27 March 2008

Dear Mr Molerro,

Thank you for your letter of 19 March addressed to the Foods Standards Agency (FSA) which was received today.

I am afraid that this is an issue that falls outside the FSA remit and which we cannot comment on.

I wish you and Mrs Molerro luck with your search for "Wet Food sludge" for those "anxious" pigs in their pens.

It just leaves me to wish you, Mrs Molerro, Tosti, Amphora and Rizzo all the best for the future.

Regards

Graham Buckley
Parliamentary Liaison

INVESTOR IN PEOPLE

Food Standards Agency, Aviation House, 125 Kingsway, London WC2B 6NH
Switchboard 020 7276 8000

Park View Road
Ealing
London W5
March 3rd, 2008

Graeme Paul Knowles Esq.
Dean of St Paul's
The Chapter House
St Paul's Churchyard
London EC4M 8AD

Dear Sir Graeme

Please may I and Mrs Molerro extend our congratulations on your recent installation into one of the top roles in the C of E, as Dean of St Paul's.

I imagine you were as appalled as I was when both lying in our respective beds listening to the Today programme on BBC Radio 4 last Wednesday morning. On came Aunty's religious affairs correspondent to announce that as part of its "Outreach 2000" programme, the Church of England is planning "affiliation" with the Druidical Council in 2009, with a view if all goes smoothly to full-blown merger probably by the start of the fiscal year 2010/11.

I thought my ears must be deceiving me! Surely the whole notion of Church and State unified as if one under HM Her Majesty the Queen is undermined by a druidical presence when these austere and ominous figures, who practice possible necromancy and frequently live in Epping Forest and Cheam, might be eligible for some of the top jobs in Church circles?

The whole drift of the church seems to be away into the sidings, not worrying about God and his Works but pulling any old lumber aboard. But for what, Dean? For the sake of being "Cool", and "Wivvit". When I saw that Chief Constable in Swansea being sworn in as a druid not long back I realised the game was up. Yes it was only Wales, but things could spread to England where the C of E still operates. Anyway how's the police officer ever going to square it with the lodge?

Frankly with steel bands in Gloucester Cathedral and smoking of the noxious weed openly indulged in at matins one can only guess where this is all going to end.

Goats and monkeys! How do we stop the rot Milord? I realise you only recently acquired the sheriff's badge as it were. But please consider whether there is not a case for capital punishment for those ready to surrender nearly 3,000 years of Christianity in the UK.

I should be grateful for your views, however extreme they may be. They could well found the basis of a sermon and so could quite easily be recycled.

I would be happy to assist with the ending, which can so often be the tricky bit in order to make sense.

Yours sincerely

R Molerro (Signor)

ST PAUL'S CATHEDRAL

The Deanery, 9 Amen Court, London EC4M 7BU

5/4/08

From The Dean of St Paul's
The Rt Revd Graeme Knowles

Dear Sister Moreno,

Thank you for your letter dated 3rd March 2008

I don't have any comment to make on your letter.

With all good wishes,

Yours, as ever,

Dean of St Paul's

END OF CORRESPONDENCE

Facsimile:020 7332 0298
Website: www.stpauls.co.uk

MOLERRO'S MENAGERIES

Park View Road
Ealing
London W5
February 16th, 2008

The Senior Curator
The Hastings Museum of Natural History
Johns Place
Bohemia Road
Hastings TN34 1ET

Dear Sir

As a top expert in small insects could you please help with an important enquiry?

Last Saturday afternoon, about 2.35pm, Mrs Molerro and I were working down the pens in the menageries. The Mrs (Rosetta) was attending to the buffalo, Simon, who has had quite a sore throat due to the recent cold snap.

As the wife was raking through the beast's mane I suddenly heard a massive howl, which was the unmistakable sound of Mrs M in extremis.

"Get this thing off me etc!!" she was yelling. Immediately I noticed a very strange little creature, looking half fish, half insect and possibly half something else, attached firmly to her forearm, sucking out the blood with an odd look on its face. Dexterously I flicked it off the wife, and into a bucket of goat feed beside her.

We transported the little beast back into the house and popped it in a shoe box where it has lain ever since, with some lettuce. Closer examination revealed a critter the likes of which we've never seen before. Various experts including the St Johns Ambulance have come round, and all are confounded. It seems to have two heads, and 12 or 13 legs, all different colores, and a small tail.

Mrs Schneider from No. 22 is certain this is the famous Missing Link from the books.

I am attaching the creature to the bottom of this letter. It is very precious and unique. Please don't lose it. Can you tell us whether we're onto something, and whether it might be worth anything?

Hoping to hear soon. All the best.

Yours sincerely

R Molerro (Mr)

PS: Please let's have it back when you've finished with it.

HASTINGS & MUSEUM ART GALLERY

Johns Place, Bohemia Road
Hastings, East Sussex
TN34 1ET

tel 0845 274 1052
fax 01424 451165

Mr R. Molerro
53a Park View Road
Ealing
London
W5

Dear Mr Molerro,

Thank you for your letter of 16 February. I am very flattered that you contacted us all the way down here in Hastings with your insect enquiry rather than going to the Natural History Museum.

However, I have bad news. Your little missing link is probably even now working its way through the postal system of this country. It has clearly made a bid for freedom and all I am left with is a bit of sellotape, a smudge of brown and a mysterious hole in the corner of the envelope.... I am very disappointed not to see the beast, especially as your description was so vivid.

If it makes its way here I will let you know, otherwise I am sorry I am unable to help.

Yours sincerely,

C. Walling

Cathy Walling
Assistant Curator

Hastings Borough Council
tel 0845 274 1066
minicom 01424 781755

Calls to 0845 numbers cost max 5p per min from BT, other providers may vary.

Old Town Hall Museum
High Street, Hastings
East Sussex TN34 1EW

tel 0845 274 1053

www.hastings.gov.uk

MOLERRO'S MENAGERIES

Park View Road
Ealing
London W5
February 25th, 2008

Ms Cathy Walling
The Assistant Curator
The Hastings Museum of Natural History
Johns Place
Bohemia Road
Hastings TN34 1ET

Dear Ms/Professor Walling

Many thanks for your lettre of 21 Febuary. We didn't try the Nat. Hist. Museum as Mrs Molerro said they'd probably muddle up our missing link with all the other critters.

The Mrs went slightly mental when she saw your epistle where it disclosed the loss of the tiny missing missing link which had been specially taped to the bottom of my lettre by the Mrs herself. **She can't understand how it's gone missing considering it was sleeping when it set off with its envelope into the letterbox only last week.** Anyway I told her she should have recorded delivery'd the beast considering she did when she sent her electric curlers back to Boots which didn't get lost.

As most people working in museums have beards could you check inside them quite carefully eg the Curator possibly? Or the gent who opens the post. Can you also look behind the bin by the desk in case the tiny link leapt out and hid somewhere.

Have you got any other missing links down in Hastings? We could send a small reptile next time or even a snake. Anyway Uncle Norman's foot was attacked by a dogfish last summer down at Bexhill-on-Sea.

Simon's quite upset too.

Hoping to hear soon.

All the best

Yours sincerely

R Molerro (Signor)

PS: Here's hoping the miniscule link's caught up with the envelope by now.

HASTINGS &
MUSEUM
ART GALLERY

Johns Place, Bohemia Road
Hastings, East Sussex
TN34 1ET

tel 0845 274 1052
fax 01424 451165

Mr R Molerro,
Park View Road
Ealing
London W5

Dear Mr Molerro,

Thank you for your letter of 25 February – I apologise for the delay in replying to you.

As you suggested, I have asked all those members of staff with beards – the male ones anyway – to check carefully for your missing link. I'm afraid there was no sign of it, although we did find paperclips, rubber bands and what we think might be a fossil. The Curator was not too pleased when I passed on your request to her.

We specialise in missing links in Hastings, and can even claim part of the blame for Piltdown Man. Otherwise we can also offer you Grey Owl and the Hastings Rarities among other great mysteries of the last century.

If Simon the bison ever feels lonely, we have a recreation of the plains of North America, where he would feel very much at home, although I feel I should warn you that we also have the mounted head of a bison on display.

I hope Uncle Norman's foot is better after his dogfish attack – that's what comes of paddling at Bexhill.

Let us know if you have anything else to be identified, and next time may I suggest you use stronger tape.

Yours sincerely,

Cathy Walling

Cathy Walling
Assistant Curator

END OF CORRESPONDENCE

Hastings

Hastings Borough Council
tel 0845 274 1066
minicom 01424 781755

Calls to 0845 numbers cost max 5p per min from BT, other providers may vary.

Old Town Hall Museum
High Street, Hastings
East Sussex TN34 1EW

tel 0845 274 1053

www.hastings.gov.uk

135

MOLERRO'S MENAGERIES

Park View Road
Ealing
London W5
March 23rd 2008

Tony Hunter Esq – Chief Executive
North East Lincolnshire Council

Dear Your Highness

Hello, I'm Mr Molerro. Could you help with a problem concerning an elderly relative?

Great Aunt Maud, the wife's granmamma's sister, is becoming something of a burden. The old bird's shacking up with us at present in the outhouse beside the pigeon shed. She's permanently confined to a wheelchair and despite having now clocked up 101 years she's showing no signs of packing it in. We reckon she's good for another 3 to 4 years or say 5,000 miles max but she's causing some upset and fright to the critters in the surrounding pens and cages, esp the marmosets who are quite timid during the seasonal mating displays etc.

Auntie Maud worked her way up from hatcheck to Tiller girl in about 1920-something, and was promoted to nymph for the 1926 season at the Windmill Theatre. She met Great Uncle Ted just after, when he was still in the goatfood racket. No sooner had he made an honest woman of her but he was posted to Borneo, where they lived in the jungle together near the natives. Their neighbours ate allsorts (dogs, rats etc) and quite a few were cannibals. It was a steep learning curve for the young lovebirds but Maud seemed to bond with the pygmies and certainly cuisine round at Maud and Ted's place back in Blighty years later was a voyage into the unknown.

Sadly Ted pegged out one Sunday in about the 1940s. The wife's ma managed to wangle the old dear into Sunnyviews Old Folks Home. However something odd happened and she was booted out after Mavis Hiplock in the next room disappeared suddenly. Matron said Aunt Maud hadn't been eating up her meals properly. Unfortunately the authorities later found Mavis's woollen booties under Aunt Maud's mattress. (They also found something unpleasant in the woodshed at Christmas).

Hoping you can re-house the old trout for us. We thought she'd blend in quite well with the locals around the hotspots of Lincs. She loves bingo and wrestling and a certain amount of horseplay. There are a couple of downsides: we wouldn't call her demented exactly but she constantly refrains lines from 1960s TV shows, such as –

"5,4,3,2,1 – Thunderbirds are GO!" , and *"Book 'em Danno!"*

She also needs to be near a telly that's showing either *Terminator* or *Die Hard*. Or *Homes under the Hammer*, with Martin Roberts and Lucy Alexander.

Hoping to hear soon.

Yours sincerely

R Molerro (Mr)

PS: Unfortunately she is also inseparable from her pet sheep, Fungus, who is permanently tethered to the wheelchair.

NORTH
EAST
LINCOLNSHIRE
C O U N C I L
www.nelincs.gov.uk

Chief Executive
Tony Hunter

Our Ref: AJH/ST

1 October 2008

Mr R Molerro
Park View Road
Ealing
LONDON
W5 2JF

Dear Mr Molerro,

Thank you for your very enjoyable and amusing letter. I assume this is not a serious request but if by any chance I am wrong, please let me know and we will, of course, seek to assist!

Yours sincerely

Tony Hunter
Chief Executive

MOLERRO'S MENAGERIES

Park View Road
Ealing
London W5
Septembre 27th., 2008

Dr Ros De'ath
University of Bristol
Office F1
12 Berkeley Square
University Road
Bristol BS8 1SS

Dear Dr De'ath

Hello, I am Mrs Molerro and the proprietor of Morello's Menageries (estd. 1972). We run successful lines in mammals, rodents, insects, gastropods and ruminants. And flightless avians.

As part of a diversifrication me and Mr Molerro are founding an offshoot of the main menageries operation. The idea is for the humane despatch into oblivion of any creatures and beasts who feel they've had enough, or who've been injured by being compressed by larger animals accidentally sitting on them etc. Or are just feeling out of sorts and no light at the end of the funnel. In other words an animal extinction agency, ie for let's say a toad who fancies a bit of euthanasia, a goat who sees no point in it all anymore, or a lemming who just wants to speed things up. The possibilities are endless! (To prevent abuse all junior applicants must be accompanied by a responsible adult).

The new operation will be situated tastefully in the old pigeon sheds at the bottom of the back garden, beside the rhubarb patch.

We were thinking of calling the new unit something like *"Dr Death's"*. So I thought we'd write and check you're OK with this, especially as we might be opening up a branch in your area.

We planning on a cheery strapline like *"Your Gateway into the Great Unknown"*.

Hoping to hear soon. Apologies we're Italain etc.

Yours sincerely

Rosetta Molerro (Mrs)

PS: Just wondering if you'd agree to become a Trustee of the extermination bureau, so we can plant your name across the top of the leaflets etc?

Dr. Ros Death,
University of Bristol,
12 Berkeley Square,
University Road,
Bristol
BS8 1SS

Mrs Rosetta Molerro,
Park View Road,
Ealing,
London,
W5 2JF

October 1st 2008.

Dear Mrs Molerro,

Thank you for your letter and kind invitation to become involved in your business, however there are a few issues that concern me. Firstly, on a professional level, having spoken to the director of my department we feel there maybe a conflict of interest between having my name associated with your business as opposed to my research interests. I am concerned that future collaborations maybe put at risk if animal loving colleagues learn of my association with the extermination bureau.

Secondly, on a more personal level, I am not comfortable with the idea of euthanasia. I am worried that it might be an easy way out for a pet owner who no longer wants to look after their animal, who finds cleaning up snail trails messy, the daily exercising of their rat tiring or feeding their mammal too much to bear. As I was brought up as a catholic and having attended a convent school, I believe that all life is precious, be it mammal or gastropod.

Maybe a better idea could be a helpline for pet owners who are finding the daily struggle of looking after their dependents too much, perhaps the Francistans (after St. Francis- the patron saint of animals). However, I do understand that this will not help those unfortunate cases where they are too squashed to continue, and feel that in these cases I can think of no better destination than your old pigeon sheds.

I regret therefore that I am unable to sanction the association of my name with this venture, but wish you all the best with your enterprises.

Yours Sincerely,
Dr. Ros Death.

P.S. You might want to run this past the RSPCA.

MOLERRO'S MENAGERIES

Park View Road
Ealing
London W5

Septembre 27th, 2008

General Sir Roger Wheeler GCB CBE
The Constable of the Tower of London
The Tower of London
Tower Hill
London EC3N 4AB

Dear My Lord

Hello. I am Mr Molerro, an Italian gent and proprietor with Mrs Molerro of the *Molerro's Menageries* (estd. 1972). Ours is a happy little business, housing lots of beasts including sheep, goats, gerbils, buffalo and emus, and lots else besides.

We have visitors from all over the Uk, and parts of Wales. Also Spain, Allemagne, New Zealand and Gib. We also lend out beasts and creatures from the menageries to zoos and bunny parks etc.

Mrs Molerro says we wonder if you'd like to replenish your menageries which have got a bit depleted. I understand you have lots of rooks, but these days hardly any big cats or reindeers.

Would you be interested in hiring out a couple of leopards and say a cheetah? Also the wife says we could chuck in a capercaille and some ocelots. I personally also think a herd of mongeese roaming the battlements in the early autumn sunshine would be a remarkable spectacle.

It's all top class stock as befits a historic settlement, rather than the downmarket critters Terry Shrimpton used to try palming off on the stately homes of England until Lord Bath caught up with him last spring at Betty Threlfall's Organic Donkey Fair in Torquay.

We can arrange delivery of a van load of "samplers" in no time. We'll back up the Rascal to the edifice then let the beasts out the trailer and usher them in. May I suggest entry through the Lion Gate and not Traitors' Gate.

Your beefeaters are welcome to check over the stock under your supervision My Lord to ensure there is not a spot of mange etc.

Unless we hear we'll assume all is well so please expect me and Mrs M one Sunday afternoon in October say around 2pm, so the whole team will be bedded in in good time for the Christmas season.

All the best

Yours sincerely

R. Molerro (Mr)

PS: Do you still administer discipline etc at the Tower? Please reply to me, not the wife.

24 October 2008

Mr R Molerro

Molerro's Menageries

Park View Road

Ealing

London

W5

Historic Royal Palaces is the
independent charity that looks
after the Tower of London,
Hampton Court Palace, the
Banqueting House, Kensington
Palace and Kew Palace. We help
everyone explore the story of
how monarchs and people have
shaped society, in some of the
greatest palaces ever built.

We receive no funding from the
Government or the Crown, so
we depend on the support of
our visitors, members, donors,
volunteers and sponsors.

Dear Mr Molerro,

Thank you for your letter of September 27th addressed to General Sir Roger Wheeler GCB CBE. Mrs Molerro is quite correct in thinking we have few animals here other than the ravens. This is, however, not so much because the stock is depleted but because it has moved. In 1831-32 those animals of the Tower Menagerie belonging to the Crown were presented to the newly established zoological society of London and transferred to their zoo in Regent's Park. I am not aware if London Zoo is in need of any sheep, goats, gerbils, buffalo or emus but I dare say you could ask.

With regard to the administration of discipline at the Tower I should perhaps clarify that this was always on behalf of the State and never for the benefit of private clients.

I would like to take this opportunity to mention that the Tower of London receives no Government or Crown funding. We are run and maintained by Historic Royal Palaces, an independent charity. The operation of the Tower and the conservation of its historic buildings and fabric are funded wholly by the income the charity generates from visitors, corporate entertainment and private donation. Should you wish to become part of this worthy cause, a cheque for £38 made out to Historic Royal Palaces can secure you the opportunity to visit not only the Tower of London but also Hampton Court Palace, Kew Palace, Kensington Palace and the Banqueting House. I enclose an application form.

Yours sincerely

Dick Harrold

Colonel R E Harrold OBE
Deputy Governor
HM Tower of London

Historic Royal Palaces
HM Tower of London, London, EC3N 4AB
Tel +44(0)844 482 7777 (Contact Centre) www.hrp.org.uk
Historic Royal Palaces is a Registered Charity (No. 1068852) and Historic Royal Palace Enterprises Ltd, a company registered in England (No. 3418583).
The registered office and address for service of both bodies is Hampton Court Palace, Surrey, KT8 9AU.

INVESTOR IN PEOPLE

MOLERRO'S MENAGERIES

Park View Road
Ealing
London W5
December 31st, 2010

Mr Tote – Managing Director
Tote
Douglas House
Tote Park
Chapel Lane
Wigan WN3 4HS

Dear Mr Tote

I write at the instance of the wife (Mrs Molerro) who is an avid animal lover, and co-proprietor (with me) of *Molerro's Menageries*.

I was transfixed by the Grande Nationale horse spectacle at Aintree racecourse up north earlier this year on the telly.

The Mrs also thought the race was quite good. But she felt it could be improved. Mrs Molerro is firmly of the view that it's wrong to penalise horses who romp home well clear of the herd just because they've got no driver left on top. After all, (the wife argues), why should the hoss cop it just cos the driver fell off the back through his own neglect or inattention, probably while taking a call on his mobile or waving to the crowd?

The wife further considers the sight of acres of horses rushing round the course together becomes somewhat monotonotonous, a great horde of brown moving along in a lump, rather like sheep which if there's too many of them can send you to sleep.

Mrs Molerro is convinced she's hit on the solution. She recommends that at next year's off you admit Doreen, her zebra from the menageries. The nag may start slowly, but goes very nicely on firm ground, especially with a little dab of English mustard on the rear end (bullseye area).

If this went well, the following year maybe you could slip in some of the wife's other beasts for variety such as the ostrich, or a kangaroo (which could be quite effective over the sticks). Or a cheetah, to encourage everyone.

Mrs Molerro feels these initiatives could open up the betting side and make the race all that more lively, and also better reflect the diverse society we live in in today's Britain.

Hoping to hear soon. Apologies we're Italian.
HappyNew Year etc
Yours sincerely

R. Molerro (Mr)

PS: Maybe forget the mustard idea as they do go faster. But not in a straight line.

tote

totesport   **tote**pool

Mr R Molerro
Park View Road
Ealing
London
W5 2JF

Tote Park
Chapel Lane
Wigan
WN3 4HS

(T) 0800 666 100
(F) 01942 617632
(E) mknowles@tote.co.uk
(W) totesport.com

10 January 2011

Dear Mr Molerro

I refer to your letter dated 31st December regarding the Grand National.

At the outset, may I thank you for your comments which I have to say have caused considerable amusement in this office. Having read your remarks several times, I am still unsure whether your suggestions are tongue-in-cheek or meant for serious consideration. Either way, I am afraid that your correspondence is ultimately addressed to the wrong authority. Whilst the tote is responsible for taking bets on the Grand National, we have no control over the nature of the race, nor which animals compete, nor the manner in which horses who lose their jockey's are handled under the rules of racing. I am afraid that those are matters for the various racing authorities rather than ourselves.

Regardless of this, may I again thank you for writing and wish you and Mrs Molerro a happy New Year. I hope that, with or without any changes, you will both enjoy this year's Grand National when it is run on 9th April.

Kind regards.

Yours sincerely

Malcolm Knowles
Customer Services Director

END OF CORRESPONDENCE

Park View Road
Ealing
London W5

January 2nd, 2011

The Chief Executive
The Halle Orchestra
The Concerts Society
Bridgewater Hall
Manchester M1 5HA

Dear Sir or Madam

Very best wishes for the New Year.

Over the past 25 years I've been touring the country with my orchestra of highly
talented musicians, performing at all sorts of venues like parks, clubs and church halls.

Under my direction we now feel ready to take on a turn at the same venue as one of
the top orchestras – the Halle!   There are a total of 37 of us, all shapes and sizes and
with a massive repertoire of all types – ballads, operas, romances and baroques etc.

We normally pack out our gigs several times over, with massive queues winding
round and round the building a few times over. We always get top billings in the local
press, possibly because we perform in the altogether (starkers) as part of our
commitment to a non-textile world of arts being a condition of our grant from the
Lottery Fund.

If you've got any slack over say Feb or March we should be able to slot in at the Hall.
I should be so pleased to know shortly. Our Rigoletto is superb, and they still talk
fondly of our Cosi Fan Tutte .

Maggie Trimbell has sprained her fetlock again so may need to be put down and
replaced if you happen to have a timpanist going spare.

Hoping all's in order. Look forward to hearing.

All the best

Yours sincerely

Rosetta Molerro (Mrs)
Conductor and lead flute

HALLÉ
MUSIC DIRECTOR SIR MARK ELDER CBE
WWW.HALLE.CO.UK

Mrs Rosetta Molerro
Park View Road
Ealing
London
W5 2JF

Wednesday, 05 January 2011

Dear Mrs Morello

Thank you for your letter, I greatly enjoyed reading its contents.

While the Hallé is resident in the Bridgewater Hall – we do not programme others to play in it. If you are looking to display your talents more fully on the stage of Manchester's home of international music, the person you should contact is Mr Peter Davison, who is the Artistic Planner at the Hall.

Alas both of our timpanists are fully engaged, so let's hope Maggie makes it back into the paddock.

With best wishes

Yours sincerely

John Summers

John Summers

Principal Sponsor

Major Sponsor

Major Sponsor

Hallé Concerts Society   Telephone 0161 237 7000   Patron HRH The Countess of Wessex   Hallé Concerts Society is a registered charity
The Bridgewater Hall   Facsimile 0161 237 7029   Chairman David McKeith   number 223882 and a company limited by
Manchester M1 5HA   Box office 0161 907 9000   Chief Executive John Summers   guarantee registered in England number 62753

Park View Road
Ealing
London W5

January 8th, 2011

Mr Peter Davison Esq
The Artistic Planner
Bridgewater Hall
Manchester M1 5HA

Dear Mr Davison

I believe we once met at the Betty Trask Tea Rooms in York. I recall you arrived on a penny farthing wearing a top hat and a tuba, ordered scones and mint cakes for everyone present which we thoroughly enjoyed, and told jokes all afternoon. But then hadn't got a shekel to meet the bill. We had a long chat whilst washing up the bone china together in the kitchen.

I am the General Manager (and Artistic Planner) of the MNO here in London. My expanding troupe of travelling musical artistes and artisans are planning our Spring and Summer season of performances, focusing on the North West. You have been strongly recommended by John Summers of the Halle as the senior honcho at the renowned Bridgewater Hall as having an interest in contemporary artistic events with a nudist aspect. A speciall copy of his lettre is attached.

I should be most grateful if you could advise any dates you may have available at BH for a Molerro's extravaganza.

Hoping to hear soon.

Please mark your envelope clearly "Nude Orchestra".

Yours sincerely

Rosetta Molerro (Mrs)
Conductor and lead flute
(and Artistic Planner)

P.S. If you still play the tuba we could fit you in the midfield, or in a defensive role.

P.P.S. Please advise the heating arrangements.

Mrs. Rosetta Molerro
Park View Road
Ealing
London W5

THE **bridgewater** HALL

11 February 2011

Dear Mrs. Molerro,

I was grateful for your letter of 8 January which requested an opportunity to expose your talents on the platform of Manchester's famous Bridgewater Hall.

I regret to say that due to a breakdown in the hall's production of hot-air, nude performances are currently not possible. Cold floors mean cold feet. However, we might fit you into our flimsy swimsuit series, which has not been popular with our resident orchestras. For some reason they have accused us of being "cheap" and "unreasonable". However, the public have embraced these concerts with open arms and assorted beachwear.

I advise all promoters at the hall to choose their repertoire carefully to avoid over-excitement, especially in a public place. Conductors must be appropriately attired at all times and bring their own batons. Musicians must carry hockey sticks and climbing ropes, otherwise escape is impossible.

You may surmise that I am in fact letting you down gently and suggesting that you try Old Trafford Football Stadium where they are more used to acts of exhibitionism. The idea of a nude orchestra is certainly intriguing and potentially entertaining, although perhaps the eye will take precedence over the ear. For this reason, I would be failing to uphold my standard, if I invited you to play.

Do you by chance perform Salomé's *Dance of the Seven Veils* by Richard Strauss? This may allow the audience to get used to the idea of orchestral nudity without the shock of immediate full frontal presentation.

with very best wishes,

Peter Davison
Artistic Consultant
The Bridgewater Hall, Manchester

END OF CORRESPONDENCE

Lower Mosley Street, Manchester M2 3WS   WEB SITE: www.bridgewater-hall.co.uk   TEL: +44 (0)161 950 0000   BOX OFFICE: +44 (0)161 907 9000
FAX: +44 (0)161 950 0001   BOX OFFICE FAX: +44 (0)161 907 9001   BOX OFFICE EMAIL: box@bridgewater-hall.co.uk
THE BRIDGEWATER HALL IS MANAGED BY: SMG Europe Holdings Limited, M.E.N. Arena, Victoria Station, Manchester M3 1AR   REGISTERED IN ENGLAND 5058259

MOLERRO'S MENAGERIES

Park View Road
Ealing
London W5
January 2nd, 2011

Andrew Rosindell Esq. MP
House of Commons
Westminster
London SW1A 0AA

Dear Mr Rosindell

The wife, Mrs Molerro (Rosetta) always has a hatful of ideas before breakfast - and
here's the latest.

The Mrs has devised a package known as **Celebrity Pet Swap**. The plan's quite
simple: recognising the limited time famous people have to go out looking for animals,
with just a phone call stars can switch their moggies, mutts and other beasts with a
specially selected critter or two from the *Molerro's Menageries* for a couple of weeks.

The idea is "animal life enrichment": the lucky beast gets to be away from the
celebrity for a while so it can be "rested" from the cameras, action and flashbulbs etc,
and, as the years of stress start falling away here in rural Ealing, can calm down and
begin to "rediscover" him/her/itself all over again.

We find that all the creatures greatly benefit from this relaxation, with lots of
opportunities to forge lifelong friendships and with that, the chance of spiritual
fulfilment.

We should be very pleased to take over your nice old pooch for a spell in and around
our pens, getting to know the locals and perhaps getting out of him/its-self a bit.

As you may miss your mutt or mogg, to fill that gap we can lend you one of a range
of alternative critters from our "lists" for the duration. Next week for example, we've
got a stoat, 4 lemmings, a gecko and a rather interesting crested iguana. Failing that,
we have a goat, and also a sheep which should be back shortly from one of your
parliamentary colleagues.

Should you need a reference on our service, Lord Archer has recently stated that
"*Molerro's is the finest celebrity pet swap service I have ever encountered*"; and
Betty Boothroyd still raves about the new lease of life our arrangements have given
her little poodle.

Look forward to hearing shortly. Remember: we're just a phone call away.

Please note that for data protection reasons we are **unable** to reveal the identity of the
beasts the stars choose to borrow.

Yours sincerely

R Molerro (Mr)

**Could we come to demonstrate at your constituency on 22 January? See you then
unless you prefer a different date. Apologies for the Inglis.**

Andrew Rosindell M.P.

Member of Parliament for Romford

House of Commons, LONDON, SW1A 0AA

Rosetta Molero
Park View Road
Ealing
London
W5

Monday 31st January 2011

Dear Rosetta,

Thank you ever so much for writing to me about your 'Celebrity Pet Swap' and for inviting me to take part with my dog, Buster.

It certainly sounds like a jolly idea; however I regret that it would not be practical for me to take part at the moment.

Buster lives with my elderly mother in Romford, whilst I live during the week in a flat in central London. I am afraid neither of us would be able to accommodate anything larger or more exotic in our homes.

Nevertheless, I am grateful to you for thinking of me and I have every hope that the scheme will be a great success!

With every good wish,

Yours sincerely

Andrew Rosindell

Andrew Rosindell M.P.

 M.P.'s Advice & Information Centre

MOLIERRO'S MENAGERIES *(ESTD. 1978)*

Park View Road
Ealing
London W5
March 18th, 2011

Whoever's in charge
Debenhams
1 Welbeck Street
London W1G 0AA

Dear Sir or Madame

I write to respectfully request some assistance from you as the leading retailers of contemporary fragrances on the Hi Street.

Me and Mr Molierro run a small private zoo and menageries here in Ealing which is an A1 establishment of high repute.

In April we hold our annual Open Day for various celebrities to attend and admire the beasts and insinuate themselves with respect to the critters. We are very honoured this year that amongst the stars will be le Duc de Montalban et Montaigne and his gracious Duchesse, who are arriving specially from Paris for the extravaganza.

The little problem we face is that the aroma from some of the pens and cages may be offensive to the nostrils of their Majesties with respect to the stench emanating from the beasts. So we wish to acquire from you some appropriate fragrances to try to blot out the worst horrors, we felt with the following emphases:

1 for the big cats, something with a wild and earthy tone, possibly evoking hints of nutmeg, cypress wood and bergamot.

2 for Derek the donkey, a casual and relaxed scent with an easy peachy aftertone, blending notes of mandarin and bay. Intense, spicy, subtle and deep.

3   for the goats and sheep, something lively and mischievous, with a luscious scent of freshly mown grass, and long lasting in case they wander off into the allotments. Maybe eau de toilette with a vaporiseteur for easy application.

4   We feel the meerkats could partner well with a grand cru de luxe, something woody, complex and round with magnolia and farmyard highlights.

5   heavy musk for the gibbons.

6   For the hippos almost anything as long as it's full bodied – and lots of it. Intense and overpowering, with citrusy overtones on the high notes for the lady hipps. Anyway, anything to get rid of the stench before they arrive*

We await your expert recommendations. Hoping to hear soon. Apologies for being Italian etc.

Yours sincerely

Rosetta Molierro (Mrs)

* a couple of buckets of Brut might do it.

DEBENHAMS

1 Welbeck Street
London W1G 0AA

Mrs R Molierro
Park View Road
Ealing
London
W5

25th March 2011

Dear Mrs Molierro

Thank you for your letter dated the 18th of March.

How very exciting to hear of the visit of the le Duc and Duchesse de Montalban et Montaigne, to your Ealing menageries.

I would imagine it will be a once in a lifetime experience for all concerned so can more than understand your desire to create the right atmosphere.

We would normally recommend that the customer visit our store in order to sample our fragrances to determine whether the product is suitable or indeed strong enough. I would however discourage you from bringing livestock into Oxford Street at present as we have major road works which would not be conducive to an easy passage.

I have discussed your predicament with a very experienced aroma specialist who also, unless I have misunderstood, happens to have wildlife. She was of the opinion that the aristocracy would be too polite to mention any overpowering whiffs and would simply smile and move on to the next exhibit.

All in all we think that it is probably best to leave things as nature intended and maybe proffer a fragrant nosegay or scented handkerchief to your esteemed guests so that they may shield their senses from anything untoward or unpleasant.

We are sorry we have not been able meet your requirements on this occasion but please bear us in mind for future purchases.

Yours sincerely

Paul Cavanagh
Manager
Customer Relations

Debenhams Retail plc. Registered in England and Wales. Company no. 83395. Registered office 1 Welbeck Street, London W1G 0AA.

Park View Road
Ealing
London W5

5 March 2011

The Head of Talent Spotting
Liverpool Football Club
Anfield Road
Liverpool L4 OTH

Dear Sir

Hail to the World's Greatest Soccer Club innit?!   Up the Liverpools!!

I'm hoping you may like an idea I've had at last. Last weekend I was kicking a football around the back garden with our youngest, Rizzo (7), and a couple of his friends, Stompie and Melrose. Suddenly the back door flew open, and the wife (Rosetta) in her apron, bedroom slippers and hair curlers, stormed down the lawn, nobbled Stompie, steered the ball round Melrose, then blasted it past Rizzo into the back of a gaping net!

Wearing a long soccer scarf in your club's colours (which she found on the bus the previous day) the Mrs then did about 5 laps of honour round the garden, punching the air and gesturing wildly to an imaginary crowd. Then without a further word she jogged back into the kitchen to finish cooking the scones.

I understand your players each earn approx £100,000 per week (min). As the Morello family finances are a bit tight at present, could I offer Mrs M's services in a forward position in your team line up for the rest of the season? She may be a bit of a carthorse around the kitchen, and at 15 stone plus she's not good in the air, but as stated she can hoof a ball up the garden, over the back fence and into the allotments with the best of them.

Mrs M is a colossal talent in the making, and shown to best effect when her bunions are under control. As Derek Flange from no. 26 points out, *"a talent scout's dream find!"*

My bones tell me it could be an unbeatable combo to slot her in a forward position.

I look forward to hearing so we can discuss the details and get the deal in place well before the festive season.

As we're coming down your way could we get a family season ticquet?

Best wishes from all the family to the Mighty Reds!

RM Morello

PS: Best not mention any of this to the wife till it's all sorted. But don't shove her in the ladies' squad. I'll square any niggles with the FA

PPS: I can move a bit on the fee if this helps smooth things along etc.

Park View Road
Ealing
London W5

5 March 2011

Rt Hon Ed Balls Esq MP
Shadow Chancellor of the Exchequer
Albion Chambers
Albion Street
Morley LS27 8DT

Dear Mr Balls

Our youngest, Rizzo (aged 7), is doing a project at school on *"The Human Body"*. All the kids in Class 3 have to think up various things to do with anatomy and have been given the run of the school library by Miss Tugg to research stuff.

Rizzo isn't any good at anything at school but seems quite excited about this project so we're keeping everything crossed. He's had some help from Tosti and Amphora at home and has come up with a list of famous people who are named after body parts:

- several members of the Foot family
- Sir Thomas Legg
- Tony Hart
- Guy Hands
- Professor Richard Beard
- Viscount Head
- Patrick Back QC
- Fu Chang Chin (ex Chinese Ambassador)

Little Rizzo is hoping you will agree to go forward in the project as it means a lot to him?

Anyway all the Feet have said yes.

Hoping to hear soon.

Thank you for your time in your busy schedule.

Yours sincerely

Rosetta Molierro (Mrs)

153

March 19th 2011

The Legal Ombudsman
PO Box 15870
Birmingham B90 9EB

Dear Mr or Mrs Ombudsman

Class 3(c) at the school of our youngest, Rizzo (aged 7) are all working on a project called **"*Doing a career when you're grown up*"**.

The kids have each been reading books about different jobs and they're all very excited because Miss Tugg (class teacher) arranged for them to visit a judge in the Officious Referee's court and then said they could each think up a question and put it in a hat, then lots to do with legal things would be picked out and read out in class with the answers.

The children were quite confused at court and also the toilets weren't working. But anyway there were lots of questions about legal things. Then none of the school staff realised they knew the answers so we all had a big meeting with Mr Dilbeck B.A. (school principal) and decided we'd write an important letter to someone to do with the law. And someone told us you are quite important to do with law things and might be able to answer them.

So here's the questions:

1 Curtis (aged 6): does it make much difference what the baristas say in the room where people get told off and can the referee tell them to shut it anyway, especially if they're useless? And clip their ear?

2 Poppy (aged 5): do judges eat things in court like flying saucers and cakes?

3 Marvin (6): does the referee ever say anything if he doesn't get what the wigg-person is on about, to do with telling him not to use long words and stop acting around?

4 Seema (7): Do the judges ever practice sleeping in court or maybe pretending they're awake when they're not because it's quite boring and anyway they want to be at home watching *Homes Under The Hammer* or *Flog It!*, or their hoss is lined up for the 2.30 at Chepstow. Or is it only the juries who are allowed to fall asleep?

5 Jeffrey (5): does the man at the top who shouts at people have a real house or does he live with the other wig people in a room somewhere?

6 Courtney (7): What happens if the match is finished and it's a draw, or the referee can't make his mind up and everyone has to go home?

7 Daisy (5): I saw this big picture thing on the wall in the court with a nasty animal with a spike in its head and a mouse or lion biting it and a crown, and I wanted to go home.*

8 Norbert (7): do people come in the court to keep warm and read the books if it's snowing outside? Anyway my uncle Ted went to court cos of something to do with making a mistake with someone else's car he borrowed for a few weeks and forgot he still had it and got banged up and reckons the courts are a waist of time.

Hoping to hear soon.

Norbert's been moved to a special class called 3(f) where we hope he'll concentrate more on woodwork.

Yours sincerely

Rosetta Molierro (Mrs)

*Miss Tugg apologises that this isn't a proper question but it still came out of the hat.

Legal Ombudsman
PO Box 15870
Birmingham
B30 9EB
T 0300 555 0333

www.legalombudsman.org.uk

Mrs Rosetta Molierro
Park view Road
Ealing
London
W5 2JF

4th April 2011

Dear Mrs. Molliero,

Thank you for your letter which only got to me last week. I am glad
Rizzo's class are interested in learning about the law. I am not a lawyer
so may not be the best person to answer your questions, but I will try
anyway. I am the Chief Legal Ombudsman. That is a bit of a mouthful
as a title but really means that, if someone who has gone to a lawyer for
help then complains about what a lawyer has done (or not done) it is my
job to decide who was right. That is why the Chief Ombudsman cannot
be a lawyer, so the person who complains knows I am independent.

Curtis's Question

The job of the barrister is to help someone in a court case (called the
"client", though I do not like the word). The barrister tries to show that
the client is right, by asking questions and making speeches. However
the barrister is not allowed to say anything they know is not true.

Trying to persuade people in court is called advocacy, and the person
doing it is sometimes called an advocate. Barristers are all advocates.
So too are some other sorts of lawyer as well.

Decisions in court cases are usually made by judges and juries (which
are made up of 12 ordinary people, like parents and teachers). They
listen to what the advocates for everyone involved in the argument have
to say and this helps them decide who if right.

The judge cannot give anyone a clip round an ear, though if they have
broken the rules the judge can tell them off or punish them. But they
must say why there are punishing them.

The Legal Ombudsman is administered by the Office for Legal Complaints under the Legal Services Act 2007.

Poppy's Question

No, no-one, including the judge, should be eating, chewing or drinking in court, although sips of water are normally allowed.

Marvin's Question

Yes, if the judge does not understand what the advocate is saying he or she will ask them to explain it better. The judge will also tell the advocate if the judge thinks the advocate is wasting time or saying things he or she is not allowed to say

Seema's Question

Judges and juries must never be asleep and must always concentrate on what is being said to them to make sure they do not miss anything important. If they didn't concentrate on everything it might make their decision unfair. But Seema is right: sometimes court is a bit boring!

Jeffrey's Question

Judges and lawyers are all ordinary people; they just have a special job and have learned special things. They often have meals with each other, like in a club, but have their own homes.

The more important judges have to travel around the country a lot and they will stay together in special houses called judges lodgings when they are working too far away from home to be able to go back there after they finish work for the day.

Courtney's Question

What a good question! Court cases cannot really end in a draw. There has to be a decision in the end.

The rule is that the side in an argument that says something has to prove it. So if the police say you have stolen something they have to prove it and make the judge or jury sure you did. Or if you say the shop sold you a play station that did not work properly and you want your money back, you have to persuade the judge that this is probably right. Sometimes a jury can't make up their mind and they have to try again with another jury. But usually the judge or jury have to make a decision.

Daisy's Question

I think what you saw is the Lion & the Unicorn which are part of the Royal Arms. The Royal Arms are a sort of badge and are in the court to show that it is working on behalf of the whole country. Do not be frightened by the Unicorn: it is only a pretend animal.

Norbert's Question

As it is very important that everyone thinks the courts are fair, they are normally open to anyone who wants to go in and watch (though sometimes children are not allowed in). Of course often people are waiting for their turn may be reading while they wait.

I am sorry that Norbert's uncle thinks courts are a waste of time. However when someone loses an argument they often say they disagree with the person deciding it. A football team that loses often says the referee was a waste of time but the winning team does not agree!

People who want their arguments sorted out normally think courts are useful way to do this. So do people who want to say they haven't done anything wrong when the police say they have.

I hope this helps. Please thank all the children for heir very interesting questions.

Yours sincerely

Adam Sampson
Chief Ombudsman

END OF CORRESPONDENCE

Park View Road
Ealing
London W5

March 18th, 2011

Sir Cliff Richardson
PO Box 46c
Esher
Surrey KT10 0RB

Dear Sir Cliff

Here's hoping your well and still getting out and about a bit.

We're starting a new Cliff Richardson Fan Club to celebrate a wonderful career. Matters are well underway and to mark your 90th birthday last year we're planning a huge musical extravaganza with loads of top celebrities from the silver screen and TV goggle box and the world of the artes.

Just some of the top-ranking artistes being arranged by our old friend Sir Mackintosh Cameron will be:

- Dame Vera Lynne
- Brian Forsythe (off the Generation Games etc)
- Rolf Harris on didgeridoo and bass guitar
- Sir Val Doonican
- Melvin from it Aint Arf Ot Mum etc
- Shirley Bassy
- Lord Hudd as Widow Twankey

The whole show will be very proper, with <u>limited nudity</u>. There'll be quite a lot of sheep and a liberal sprinkling of goats too. Lord Lloyd weber has graciously agreed to provide John Prescott by special arrangement (rear end panto horse etc) and a herd of chimpanzees.

Dame Noreen Fetlock WRVS (W'don Champ 1919) will say a few words on *"getting the most out of your backhand".*

Could you then do a couple of numbers (Young Ones and Summer Holiday) before the Amazing Kardoma winds up with some juggling and snakes and a firework display?

Front of house will be c £30, £75 for the Gods.

We're also hoping for a giraffe.

Apologies we're Italain.

Yours sincerely

Rosetta Molierro (Mrs)

PS And a llama.

> Park View Road
> Ealing
> London W5
> April 5th, 2011

Ms Clare Clancy
HM Registrar of Companies
Crown Way
Maindy
Cardiff CF14 3UZ

Dear Ms Clancy

We are a small group of Hallelujah! Worshippers here in West Ealing who believe in peace and goodwill amongst everyone.

On alternate Sundays we do little "Harmony Events" around parts of the Borough of Ealing where we sit in each other's houses chanting happy melodies and telling joyful stories to cheer each other up, led by the Reverend Pritchard and his new assistant, Bunty Hinchcliffe.

We were due to have a "get to know you" session for one or two new members last Sunday 2 April at the bungalow of one of our members, Mavis Trimble (Miss), in Hillbeck Way, Greenford.

But then a distressed Mavis came on the line to Bunty, immensely upset about the signage that's gone up for a local business round the corner in Greenford Road - called the ***"Anytime Gully Sucking Company Limited"***!

Mavis was almost in tears as she explained the torment this company name had caused her, what with her rather sheltered upbringing.

As a married man of many years I am only too aware of the ways of the world and have been struggling to come to terms with this. But poor Mavis was dreadfully worried that our members, and especially newcomers, would be disturbed and put off. And we'd worked so hard to coax Mr and Mrs Bullfinch into our group too.

We believe the company concerned to be a well-meaning enterprise and we're sure they've done nothing wrong. We wrote asking if they could cover up the signs on the day, but haven't heard, and we just couldn't take the risk especially what with Mavis's angina.

It was such a shame about last Sunday. All the songs were prepared. And the nibbles.

We've rescheduled the event for 16th April and we're just hoping some common sense will prevail in this world gone mad. As you can well imagine the whole episode has been terribly distressing.

Could you please suggest what could be done? Hoping to hear soon.
Yours sincerely

R Molerro (Mrs)
PS: Just to add to the woe, Mavis has just pointed out that at the same address is another company called …. **Anytime Pumping Limited.**

Companies House
for the record

From the Chief Executive and Registrar of Companies

Mr R Molerro
West Ealing Hallelujah! Worshippers' Centre
Park View Road
Ealing
London W5

Crown Way Cardiff CF14 3UZ
Telephone 0303 1234 500
Fax 029 2038 0517
DX 33050 Cardiff
www.companieshouse.gov.uk

Date   13 April 2011

Dear Mr Molerro

Thank you for your letters of 5 April 2011 addressed to the Registrar of Companies for England & Wales, Scotland and Northern Ireland.

I am sorry to hear of the distress to your group, and also sorry that there is little we can do to help.

There is indeed a company on the Register with the name of Anytime Pumping Limited. A quick search of the internet also told me that there is a company operating from Greenford Road supplying the services of gully sucking to clear drains, empty gullies, pump out flooded areas, etc. with the name of Anytime Gully Sucking Company (gully sucker being the type of vehicle used to carry out these types of operations). This company is not registered with us and is not a limited company. If it does indeed include the word limited on the notice outside the premises in Greenford Road we can, if you wish, take this complaint forward by writing to them to have it removed. It would, however, leave the rest of their name intact which would not seem to help your group.

Maybe if Mavis understands that the work they are doing is not offensive it may, however, help with her embarrassment.

Yours sincerely

Morag Baker
Chief Executive's Correspondence Manager

Companies House is an Executive Agency of the Department for Business, Innovation and Skills (BIS)

Awarded For Excellence

WEST EALING HALLELUJAH! WORSHIPPERS' CENTRE
(Estd. 1978)

Park View Road
Ealing
London W5

June 2nd, 2011

Ms Morag Baker
HM Registrar of Companies
Crown Way
Maindy
Cardiff CF14 3UZ

Dear Ms Baker

Many thank yous for your letter of 13th April, which arrived just too late for our specially adjourned Harmony Group on 16th April.

Our members spotted that you mention that the Anytime Gully Sucking Company is not a limited company.

Surely you can't be suggesting that poor Mavis has to start putting up with **unlimited**, round-the-clock gully sucking just yards from Sweetpea Cottage?

As Reverend Pritchard points out, this is the last thing we want what with Mavis's angina and her whooping cough.

And fancy dragging drains and sewers into it too!

It's all proved too much. Mavis has had had a swoon and fallen over again.

God bless,

Yours sincerely

R Molerro (Mr)

Companies House
for the record

From the Chief Executive and Registrar of Companies

Mr R Molerro
West Ealing Hallelujah! Worshippers' Centre
Park View Road
Ealing
London W5

Crown Way Cardiff CF14 3UZ
Telephone 0303 1234 500
Fax 029 2038 0517
DX 33050 Cardiff
www.companieshouse.gov.uk

Date   15 June 2011

Dear Mr Molerro

Thank you for your letter of 2 June. I really must apologise for adding to poor Mavis's distress by gurgling on about drains and sewers in my previous letter.

I have noted your concerns about the unlimited status of the Anytime Gully Sucking Company. As there is also a limited company registered at this address, namely Anytime Pumping Limited, I am sure they can be trusted to act responsibly and cause as little distress to the precarious Mavis and your group as they possibly can. Maybe you could ask Reverend Pritchard to have a word with them to keep their pumping and gully sucking down to an acceptable level?

Once again, my apologies for any distress caused to poor Mavis, and I wish you and the other members of the Hallelujah Harmony Group continued enjoyment in your chanting and story telling.

Yours sincerely

Morag Baker
Chief Executive's Correspondence Manager

P.S. I hope this hasn't exacerbated Mavis's angina.

P.P.S. Best wishes to the Bullfinches

Awarded For Excellence

Companies House is an Executive Agency of the Department for Business, Innovation and Skills (BIS)

Park View Road
Ealing
London W5

April 15th, 2011

Mr Eric Pickles MP
House of Commons
Westminster
London SW1A OAA

Dear Mr Pickles

Please can I write to you about something?

Last April I lent you £20 (or a "monkey" as I noted you referred to it) when you approached me at Aintree racecourse during feverish betting on the Grand National. I remember the occasion vividly. You were shouting some unusual language at a group of ladies in the Royal Enclosure whilst waving a hot dog around.

You were so grateful for the loan at the time, saying it was a lifesaver as you'd given all your spare to "a good cause" in Liverpool on the way to the course. And that you'd been tipped off which hoss was going to breast the tape.

I recall you adding that " *the dosh is safe as houses – I'm a Member of Parliament*", and that I could expect it back almost before I got home.

Twelve months and several phonecalls to the HoC later …..and I'm still waiting.

The fact that your horse pitched it's rider off and fell over almost immediately the starter's flag dropp'd is hardly my fault

I would be grateful for an explanation, preferably before the end of the century.

Yours sincerely

R. Molierro (Mr)

164

The Rt Hon Eric Pickles MP

HOUSE OF COMMONS
LONDON SW1A 0AA

21 April 2011

Mr R Molierro
Park View Road
Ealing
London W5

Dear Mr Molierro

Thank you for your letter. Mr Pickles has never visited Aintree or any other racecourse and did not attend the Grand National. Mr Pickles would also never borrow money from a total stranger.

All telephone calls to this office are logged and no call has been received from you.

Yours sincerely

Lesley Gaymer
Head of Office to
The Rt Hon Eric Pickles MP
Brentwood and Ongar

Member of Parliament for Brentwood and Ongar

Park View Road
Ealing
London W5

April 23rd, 2011

Ms/Mr/Mrs Lesley Gaymer
Head of Office to Mr Eric Pickles MP
House of Commons
Westminster
London SW1A OAA

Dear Mr or Mrs Gaymer

I have just noted a small letter from yourself addressed to Mr Molierro (my husband) about Sir Pickles and the so-called monkey.

I have had a firm discussion with Mr Molierro and it turns out there is a silly mistake in that there was no monkey involved at all. Also it seems it was someone else in Parliament. And it wasn't at the Grand National. Anyway it was Catterick. Or Doncaster.

Apologies once again for this mixup.

Also there was no hot dogg.

 Yours sincerely

Rosetta Molierro (Mrs)

Park View Road
Ealing
London W5

April 7th, 2011

The Managing Director
Kimberly Clark Inc/Andrex
Douglas House
40 London Road
Reigate
Surrey RH12 9QP

Dear Sir or Madam

Today you shoved a load of toilet paper related stuff through my letter box

What's the big idea?

Is this someone's idea of a joke?

You also shoved a booklet through the door telling me to change my purchase to
"Andrex Skin Kind Toilet Tissue".

If I want advice on bog paper I'll ask for it thanks a lot. I use Bronco and I'm happy
with it.

The next thing is you'll be shoving your head up the U Bend with an advertising
leaflet while I'm sat on the throne.

Does the British Toilet Association know about this?

Yours sincerely

RM Molerro (Mr)

cc: The B.T.A.

Park View Road
Ealing
London W5

April 7th, 2011

The Director-General
The British Toilet Association
PO Box 847
Horsham
West Sussex RH12 5AL

Dear Sir or Madame

I am not familiar with the British Toilet Association but Mrs Molerro says she hopes you aren't a collection of humorists who meet up weekly in a pub to exchange schoolboy jokes about bodily functions - as suggested by your website with its constant references to your "bottom down" approach to problems.

We write in the hope that you are a serious research institute who can assist in our quest for a solution to a rather sensitive issue.

I attach a letter we have sent today to Kimberly Clark Inc regarding their insistent demands that we change our toilette paper at home.

Is it really where we've got to in this mad, mad world that people endlessly send each other things through the post about going to the toilet? Do they really have nothing better to do? When I was in the forces in Anzio the RSM told us we were bloody lucky to have a handful of leaves to finish the job, pine needles included.

Anyway if you do think the world's moved on since Bronco, and Izal won't do either, the Mrs (Rosetta) joins me in asking what you would suggest?

By the way I assume you are aware that down in sunny old St Leonard's on Sea there is a whole suburb called Lavatoria. I recommend it for your next AGM.

Yours sincerely

RM Molerro (Signor)

PS: and before you ask, yes I do wash my hands after I've been. And put the seat down again.

Kimberly-Clark Europe

28 April 2011

Mr R. Molerro
Park View Road
LONDON,
W5 2JB

Dear Mr Molerro,

Thank you for your recent letter regarding ANDREX® Skin Kind toilet tissue.

We hope you will accept our apologies for the inconvenience you have experienced. The samples and coupons were merely sent as a way for consumers to try the new product and we were sorry to hear that you did not appreciate this mailing. As a gesture of our goodwill, we are sending you a complimentary voucher in the post which can be redeemed against a future purchase of any Kimberly-Clark products, which include brands such as ANDREX®, KLEENEX® and HUGGIES®.

Thank you once again for taking the time to contact us.

Yours sincerely,

Richard Espinosa Nieto
Consumer Services Department

016087816A

MOLIERRO'S MENAGERIES

Park View Road
Ealing
London W5

April 16th, 2011

Sir Leslek Borysiewicz
Vice Chancellor - Cambridge University
The Old Schools, Trinity Lane
Cambridge CB2 1TN

Dear Sir Leslek

Oxford and Cambridge University Boat Race

Me and Mrs Molierro (Rosetta) were very disappointed to watch the Light
Blues just losing out to the other team in the boat race about a couple of weeks
back. They seemed to be smaller and weaker than yourselves and (as expected)
somewhat less intelligent, so the result was a definite surprise.

We began to wonder if they hadn't slipp'd something into your vessel before
the off such as a couple of sacks of cement and some lead piping. You seemed
to go quite nicely then sort of slid round and started going the wrong way
having misinterpretated the satnav probably.

As the Boat Race has been going for about 200 years without stopping would
it be possible to have something a bit diff'rent next year - such as a
University Goat Race?

Here at Molierro's we have an excellent variety of goats of all shapes and sizes
just like in the boats, and from all over the place like your lot as well – eg
Russian Cossack whites, Australian hardbacks, the large-horned rampant
Alpine, the British Booted Goat   and of course the tiny but spirited
Toggenbergs.

Could we bring a pile of gaots down to your office in the Transit for you to
make the selection and get them into training without delay?

Anyway if you decided you wanted to go ahead with the boats anyway next
year, the goats could still race along the edge of the river, one team on each
side, encouraged by yourself My Lord with buckets of carrots and dandelions.
And the other Vice-Chief.

We have a first-rate friendly Toggenberg in pen at present which though
slightly lame has good udders (measured at 2.4 on the British Goat Society
index). Being small and with these accoutrements the Togg could be ideal in
the cox position for the off.

Would it be ok to head up on Thursday week and bring the goats assuming it's
all still on? Hoping to hear sooner rather than later if not.

Many thanks for your help and apologies for being Italian.

Yours sincerely

R Molierro (Mr)

Matthew Moss MA
Private Secretary to the Vice-Chancellor

UNIVERSITY OF CAMBRIDGE
Vice-Chancellor's Office

Mr R. Molierro
Molierro's Menageries
Park View Road
Ealing
London W5

21 April 2011

Dear Mr Molierro.

Thank you for your letter to Sir Leszek dated 16 April 2011, concerning the University Boat Race.

Following the unsporting behaviour of the Oxford Blue Boat in winning this year's race so blatantly, Cambridge is considering jacking the whole thing in while we're ahead (80 to 76 in the series so far), and so in a sense your letter was timely.

In another sense, however, it is all now far too late – Spitalfields City Farm has been running a University Goat Race for three years, which took the wind out of our sails a bit when we discovered it (though it turns out that our goats have trounced the other lot 3-0). Had we known earlier about the Goat Race possibility, it might all have turned out differently – I don't know if patent law applies to goats, but it's a complication too far for us now.

Accordingly we've been exploring alternative sporting fixtures. We are now heavily invested in an opportunity presented to us by Mr Abalone of Abalone's Aquatics, who can secure for us the use of a nearby country estate for the racing of turtles. It's all a bit uncertain (between you and me I suspect Mr Abalone may not be all he claims to be) but if all goes to plan we hope that by 2012 the Light Greens will be taking on the Dark Greens in the first University Moat Race.

Thank you again for your splendid and thoughtful letter, and I hope this will not be too much of a disappointment.

Yours sincerely,
Matthew Moss

END OF CORRESPONDENCE

The Old Schools
Trinity Lane
Cambridge CB2 1TN

MOLIERRO PRODUCTIONS INC
(established 1989)

Park View Road
Ealing
London W5
April 8th, 2011

Wilfred Emanuel-Jones Esq
Managing Director
The Black Farmer Limited
Lansdowne House
3-7 Northcote Road
London SW11 1NG

Dear Mr Emanuel-Jones

We are a small TV production company of me and Mrs Molierro, with occasional help from Messrs Enoch and Desmond, the highly regarded but exclusive agency known for their work on the small screen in the UK and beyond. The whole family absolutely loves your products at The Black Farmer.

We are presently working on a biopic of **Wesley Snipes,** the renowned US celebrity and film star. The production is to be a *docusoap* focusing on the star's achievements both in and out of his screen roles and across the board with reference to his social and community feats and deeds. We already have funding in the form of mezzanine finance, and some great locational plans.

A lot of the casting is sorted, with several big stars already in place. However we lack a real charismatic celebrity to take the lead role as Wesley himself. We're looking for someone lean, hungry and rugged, but with a softer side too that appeals to the ladies, and can wield a gun or a bunch of flowers without losing track of the plot. In short, someone with the Wow Factor!

We 're not sure whether you feel you might wish to become a celebrity yourself but thought you should consider this lead role to help take your career to that next level.

Needless to say the rewards will be considerable, commensurate with the prestigious nature of the assignment. There will be several romantic scenes which you may quite enjoy.

We're auditioning very soon and would be most grateful for the earliest indication as to whether you feel you would like to make the jump up to the next stage. If so we can fax you an application form at once.
With best wishes

Yours respectfully

RM Molierro (Mr)

MOLIERRO PRODUCTIONS INC
(established 1989)

Park View Road
Ealing
London W5
May 15th, 2011

Wilfred Emanuel-Jones Esq
Managing Director
The Black Farmer Limited
Lansdowne House
3-7 Northcote Road
London SW11 1NG

Dear Mr Emanuel-Jones

Thank you for your recent message stating how pleased you were that we here at Molierro's Productions have considered you for the role of Wesley Snipes in the forthcoming biopic of his life and how much you admire Wes.

Unfortunately there has been an enormous response. Competition has been intense for the role and I regret to inform you that your name has not gone forward to the next round. I am sorry to disappoint you on this occasion.

However not all is lost. Not by any means. We note from your letterhead your speciality as a producer of Award-Winning Sausages, Bacon, Chicken and BBQs.

We should like to appoint you as on site caterers for the production, providing ravenous gaffers, soundies and grips with all their in-production foodie needs.

Please report to me in Caravan No 2 at 8am next Tuesday morning with a large box of BBQ buns. Don't forget to bring your own mug.

Yours sincerely

Rosetta Molierro

Rosetta Molierro (Mrs)
Head of Casting

PS: Morgan Freeman has just been appointed to play Wes.

ITALIANI A LONDRA
(founded 1973)

Park View Road
Ealing
London W5

April 12th, 2011

Carlo Ancelotti Esq.
The Manager
Chelsea Football Club
Stamford Bridge
Chelsea
London SW6 1HS

Dear Mr Ancelotti

I am writing on behalf of approximately 27,000 persons of Italian background in London who belong to *Italiani a Londra,* an informal association dedicated to helping our countrymen - and women - to find their feet in the capital, and to encourage a better understanding and appreciation of Italians over here in the UK and cultural exchanges between the two nations. In short, to foster love and harmony between us and the English.

We have a packed programme of events for the coming season, being the 150th year of Italian unity. Our showcase event, on 30 April at 7pm in the West End, will be a glittering occasion involving several top sportsmen and administrators and many celebrities including Natalie Imbruglia, Al Pacino and also we will be thrilled to have amongst us HE the Italian Ambassador to the Court of St James'. (and Rolf Harris).

We would like to ask if you could attend, as Guest of Honour. We can arrange transportations and overnight accommodation if this would assist. You would of course be on the Top Table with the celebrity guests and Rolf, and also Kenton and Delia who both sit on our Events Committee and will accompany you for the evening.

It would be a great honour to all our members to hear that you can accept the association's invitation. You will not be required to speak.

Please could you advise so that we can confirm arrangements.

Thank you very much for your time.

Yours sincerely

Rosetta Molerro (Mrs)
Secretary-General

CHELSEA FOOTBALL CLUB

Ca/jw

4th May 2011

R M MOLETTO ESQ
Park View Road
EALING
London W5

Dear Moletto,

Thank you for your recent letter regarding your Wife's previous letter of 12th April.

I am sorry for not responding to Mrs Molerro, but the letter never arrived with me and I can only assume got lost in the postal system along the way.

I note your showcase was on 30th April and hope you have a very enjoyable and successful event.

Apologies again for not attending.

Kind regards.

Yours sincerely,

Carlo Ancelotti
<u>Manager – 1st Team Coach</u>

Chelsea Football Club Ltd
Cobham Training Ground
60 Stoke Road
Stoke D'Abernon
Cobham
Surrey
KT11 3PT

www.chelseafc.com

Registered No.   1965149
Registered Office: Stamford Bridge, Fulham Road,
London, SW6 1HS

CLUB SPONSOR

KIT SUPPLIER & SPONSOR

ITALIANI A LONDRA
(founded 1973)

Park View Road
Ealing
London W5

May 6th, 2011

Carlo Ancelotti Esq.
The Manager
Chelsea Football Club
60 Stoke Road
Stoke d'Abernon
Cobham
Surrey KT11 3PT

And by fax

Dear Mr Ancelotti

Many thanks for your letter of 4 May to Mr Moletto (who is my husband, Mr Molerro).

In fact we had to postpone the whole extravaganza due to logisticals and related things like that. It's now on Saturday evening 28 May.

Anyway here's hoping you can attend as our special Guest of Honour. You will have an escort all evening with Delia and Kenton who will be in evening dress and will show you around and introduce you to the celebs. Hope you can attend with Mrs Ancelotti, or anyone else.

Also I can confirm that Rolf Harris will **not** be attending, should that assist with the decision.

Hoping to hear soon.

Yours sincerely

Rosetta Molerro (Mrs)

CHELSEA FOOTBALL CLUB

Ca/jw

12th May 2011

MRS R MOLERRO
Park View Road
EALING
London W5

Dear Mrs Molerro,

Thank you for your recent letter.

Unfortunately I already have a commitment on 28th and therefore will be unable to attend.

Thank you for the kind invitation anyway.

With best wishes.

Yours sincerely,

Carlo Ancelotti
Manager – 1st Team Coach

Chelsea Football Club Ltd
Cobham Training Ground
60 Stoke Road
Stoke D'Abernon
Cobham
Surrey
KT11 3PT

www.chelseafc.com

Registered No. 1965149
Registered Office Stamford Bridge, Fulham Road,
London, SW6 1HS

SAMSUNG
CLUB SPONSOR

adidas
KIT SUPPLIER & SPONSOR

Park View Road
Ealing
London W5

April 16th, 2011

The Senior Baker
Allied Bakeries
1 Kingsmill Place
Vanwall Road
Maidenhead
Berks. SL6 4UF

Dear Sir or Madam

I write to you as a gent (or possible lady) standing at the pinnacle of baking.

The wife, Rosetta, (15 and a half stone excluding handbag) has always enthusiastically supported the British baking industry. In fact she has thrown herself into the project with gusto over many years, with a particularly selfless commitment to the cream cakes sector, as I can confirm first-hand.

The Mrs feels some recognition is now long overdue for this exceptional level of contribution. She enquires whether she could be the star guest at your next Annual Luncheon or Dinner (or both)? She proposes making a brief speech, and in reply to be acclaimed by your President as "Toast of the Nation", followed by presentation with a Lifetime Achievement Award.

Looking forward to hearing, and to receiving a copy of the menu for perusal.

Apologies we're Italian.

Yours sincerely

R. Molierro (Mr)

ALLIED BAKERIES

CUSTOMER SERVICES
Vanwall Road, Maidenhead, Berkshire. SL6 4UF
Telephone 01628 507320 Facsimile 01628 507390

Ref: 4248708

03/06/2011

Mr Molierro
Park View Road
Ealing
London
W5

Dear Mr Molierro,

We are writing in connection with your letter regarding Rosetta your wife.

How wonderful to hear that your wife has spent many years supporting the British baking industry.
We are sure the cream cake sector would love to hear how she embraces the product and is now
practically an authority on the subject.

We, as you know produce bread, rolls, crumpets, pancakes, hot cross buns etc., and we are sure she
has sampled many of these over the years to her delight.

We also feel that recognition for her support is long overdue and if we were to have an Annual
Luncheon or Dinner we would be sure to extend an invitation to acclaim Rosetta publicly as the
"Toast of the Nation". We would have loved nothing more than to hear her extol her praises for our
products.

We can however, send as a gesture of goodwill vouchers to the value of £5.00, to enable Rosetta to
purchase product of her choice from our range.

Keep enjoying our products Rosetta.

Arrivederci

Yours sincerely,

Christine Harrington
Consumer Services Adviser

END OF CORRESPONDENCE

Allied Bakeries - A Division of ABF Grain Products Limited Registered in England No 79590
Registered Office: Weston Centre, 10 Grosvenor Street, London W1K 4QY

Park View Road
Ealing
London W5

April 23rd 2011

Professor Baron Hennessy of Nympsfield FBA
Department of History
Queen Mary - University of London
London E1 4NS

Dear Professor Hennessy, Lord

The wife (Rosetta) is helping the local primary school, which our youngest Rizzo (7) attends, to organise an end-of-term pageant on political life in Britain. It's especially to do with the Cabinet, with each child playing a cabinet minister and they have to keep secrets just like the ministers do.

The kids have to read lines out with the correct titles (eg *"Certainly Prime Minister"* and *"I entirely agree with the Secretary of State for Wales on this matter"* etc). But most of them don't know any politicians at all so the teachers are letting them use voices of stars they know off the telly.

Mr Dilbeck (Head) said you know quite a lot about things like this so here goes with the list the kids have put together:

Prime Minister (David Cameron) – Clark Kent

Nick Clegg - Cpl. Jones (don't panic! etc)

George Osborne – Kenneth Williams

Kenneth Clarke – Dame Peggy Mount

Theresa May – Charles Bronson

Liam Fox – Ronnie Corbett

Andrew Lansley CBE – Jean Claude van Damme

Chris Huhne – Jenson Button

Dr Vince Cable – Victor Meldrew

Iain Duncan Smith – Vinnie Jones

Michael Gove – John Inman

Eric Pickles – Hattie Jacques

Caroline Spelman – June Whitfield

Jeremy Hunt – Lionel Blair

Lord Strathclyde QC – Hyacinth Bouquet

Baroness Warsi – Shirley Bassy

Rt Hon Francis Maude – Lee van Cleef

Oliver Letwin – Ena Sharples

David Willetts – Popeye

Sir George Young Bart. – Sgt. Wilson

Rt Hon Dominic Grieve – Percy Thrower (bird impersonator)

Could you suggest any improvements? Sorry if we've missed anyone.

Rizzo's very upset that due to making a mess of all his class tests he's been punished by being told he's doing a non-Cabinet minister – someone I've never heard of. And can't remember anyway, (played by Norman Wisdom).

Hoping to hear soon. Apologies for being Italian etc.

Yours sincerely

R Molierro (Mr)

Professor the Lord Hennessy of Nympsfield FBA

House of Lords
Palace of Westminster
London SW1A 0PW

21 MAY 2011

Dear Mr. Molierro,

Thank you for your wonderful letter! It made me laugh out loud.

Best wishes to you and to Rozetta, Rizzo and Mr. Dilbeck.

All good wishes,

Yours sincerely,

Peter Hennessy

PS. I used to go to school in Ealing at St. Benedict's

END OF CORRESPONDENCE

ST HILDA'S SCHOOL FOR YOUNG LADIES OF REFINEMENT
(est'd 1871)

School House
Park View Road
Ealing
London W5
May 2nd, 2011

The Harlem Globetrotters
400 E van Buren
Phoenix
Arizona 85260
USA

Dear Sir or Madam

Here at St Hilda's we have been producing ladies of refinement aged 14 to 18 for well over a century, since the days of one of our first governors, William Gladstone, whose stern moral fibre and upright bearing is inculcated into all our young ladies.

Our ladies' academic attainment is second to none. But we also lay emphasis on sporting achievement, as exemplified by St Hilda herself. The girls love hockey, rounders and tennis but also netball.

We understand you have a netball team at your college with some quite good players. I have recently taken over the reins as the school's new sports mistress which is rather daunting as I've only ever taught woodwork and RE before. We'd love to offer you a fixture when we do a little visit to the States of United America in the summer, from 21 June to 9 July. Lettuce McKibbin is frightfully good at throwing the ball into an open space, and Primrose Trubshaw, at 5 foot 6 our tallest netballer, is terribly promising at catching on the move and finding the net. Sophie and Petunia are also showing signs of real promise having worked awfully hard on their skipping and hopscotch.

We've had a few snuffles round the corridors after a recent cold snap but I'm sure that's nothing a good Vick's chest rub and lots of greens can't put right! And recently we overcame St Mildred's Academy for Girls 7-5 after a really super game, and jolly well done too to all our little hens involved is all I can say.

I do look forward to hearing soon. Perhaps after the match we can treat your team to a milk shake and possibly even some flavoured ices before we bustle away to fulfil our busy timetable.

Yours sincerely

Rosetta Molierro (Mrs)
Sports Mistress and hopscotch co-ordinator

MOLIERRO'S MENAGERIES
(est'd. 1978)

Park View Road
Ealing
London W5

April 25th, 2011

The Head of Ads
Cadbury's chocolates etc
Cadbury House
Uxbridge Business Park
Uxbridge
Middlesex UB8 1DH

Dear Sir or Madam

I write on behalf of the Mrs (Mrs Molierro) who is Chief Executive of *Molierro's*, one of the finest menageries in West Ealing, where we run a tidy little operation (far better than Betty Shrimpton's *Animalworld*) and have just got in a new pile of goats, otters and terripins. And a Bactrian camel (two lumps).

The Mrs was a bit worried not to have seen that guerilla lately on your ads hammering out a tune on the drums with Phil Collinson in the background.

The wife enquires whether the gorilla is still pursuing a musical career or whether perhaps he/she/it has diversifried into Hollywood possibly? If so Mrs Molierro points out that we can offer either Delia or Kenton (also gorillas) who, although having limited experience with drums, can smash out various noises on dustbin lids, as the Mrs discovered when she playfully hid their feeding bowls last Tuesday. Mrs Molierro feels these harmonies could be harnessed into something quite promising and anyway Kenton sailed through boot camp on *Britain's Got Talent* last summer.

The wife states we can discuss terms, though if you can't afford gorillas any more we could offer a very reasonably priced chimp blasting one out on a piccolo or, slightly more melodiously, a baboon playing the harp.

If you don't insist on primates, the range is much wider. You'd be surprised what a goat can do with a saxophone given half a chance.

Naturally we'd prefer to assist on the ape side if possible. Could I mention your gorilla has something of a resemblance to the ma-in-law with those long arms and hairy complexion.

Hoping to hear soon. Please reply to me not the wife.

Yours sincerely

RM Molierro
(Deputy Head of Primates)

PS: Anyway I read somewhere that a monkey was left in a room with a typewriter for a long bank holiday weekend and produced the whole works of Shakespeer.

27 May 2011

Cadbury

Mr R M Molierro
Park View Road
LONDON
W5 2JF

Cadbury UK
PO Box 12, Bournville
Birmingham B30 2LU

consumer direct line: 0800 818181
switchboard: 0121 458 2000
fax: 0121 451 4297
web: www.cadbury.co.uk

Our Ref:- 003106805A

Dear Mr Molierro

Thank you very much for your recent letter concerning our Gorilla advertising.

I was concerned to learn that Mrs Molierro has become worried about the whereabouts of our special Cadbury Gorilla. Please reassure Mrs Molierro that he is fine and very happy having now retired from international stardom.

We have no plans to introduce any other featured animal in our current advertising – indeed our new advertising 'Clothes' has just recently been launched. No sign of the gorilla, but plenty of clothes behaving mischieveously in a charity shop.

We do appreciate you contacting us with your kind offer to source any future animals from your menagerie, please be assured we will bear this in mind for future reference.

I know Mrs Molierro may be disappointed with our response, so I've included below some fun facts about the Gorilla advertising - hope she finds them interesting.

The actor inside the gorilla suit, Garon Michael, was an experienced animatronics actor who has appeared in Congo, Instinct and Planet of the Apes. He's spent a lifetime perfecting his gorilla art with visits to observe the animals in their natural habitat, on film and in zoos. The gorilla suit was on loan from Stan Winston Studios who have also created suits and monsters for classic action films like The Terminator, Aliens, Edward Scissor Hands and Predator.

Gorillas have a dominating visual presence as the largest of the living primates. They exhibit lots of human characteristics which when applied to a human activity like drumming, means movements can look exaggerated. Its movements are also generally slow, meaning that the anticipation of waiting for the moment when the gorilla hits the drums is built up adding additional theatre and drama to the advertisement before the full music kicks in.

Your comments put me in mind of a former colleague who unceremoniously claimed he was astounded at the likeness the gorilla bore to his mother in law, adding however that the gorilla was far better on the drums than her.

Thanks again for your letter. We wish you and Mrs Molierro all the very best.

Kind regards

Jane Potts
Consumer Relations Department

END OF CORRESPONDENCE

creating brands
people **love**

MOLERRO'S MENAGERIES

Park View Road
Ealing
London W5

May 7th, 2011

Ms Alex Polizzi
Managing Director
The Hotel Endsleigh
Milton Abbot
Tavistock
Devon PL19 0PQ

Dear Ms Polizzi

May I introduce myself as Mr Molerro. We think you're excellent on the show "The Hotel Inspector" and I particularly enjoyed the episode where that Welsh chef and his plump family weren't any good and got it both barrels at the Happy Traveller.

We run a menageries up here in London having originally started in Devon, though we note you've done it the other way round.

I was interested to note from your website you have a Vietnamese pot-bellied pig in your reception area. The wife does that role for us here and also enjoys the company of visitors.

Now that we've sorted the basics with the menageries we're interested in opening a guest house which is more or less the same as a hotel anyway, as what you need is some pens or rooms and mealtimes though obviously the animals can't escape in the same way the guests can. Also you can eat them sometimes.

Do you think down south like you would be a good place for our business? We found the Devons and Cornishes quite difficult to understand as they have a different sort of language which is very slow unlike us and their culture is diff'rent to England with unusual practices.

Hoping to hear soon.

Would you be able to open our new venture please?

Many thanks for all your assistants.

Yours sincerely

R Molerro (Mr)

PS: Please reply to me not the wife.

HOTEL ENDSLEIGH

27th May 2011

Dear Mr and Mrs Molerro

I am sorry that you have not heard from Alex. I am afraid she is an extremely busy lady and is often overseas. Contrary to expectations she does not have a personal assistant and deals with all her correspondence herself which I understand is sometimes rather overwhelming!

I have of course sent your letter on to her.

I'm afraid our Vietnamese Pot-Bellied pig grew rather big for us and has now got a happy home on a children's farm. She started eating the cabling and pipe work in the hotel which was not very good for the hotel or indeed for her.

I would love to welcome you to Hotel Endsleigh during July. We are fully booked from 14 July until 17 July so I'm afraid we could not accommodate you until Monday 18th July.

With very kind regards

Helen Costello
General Manager

Milton Abbot, Tavistock, Devon PL19 0PQ
Tel: +44 (0)1822 870 000 Fax: +44 (0)1822 870 578 Email: mail@hotelendsleigh.com
www.hotelendsleigh.com

Company Registration No. 5028551 VAT Registration No. 844 2763 16
Endsleigh House Limited Registered Office: Rotherwick House, 3 Thomas More Street, London E1 9YX Registered in England.

187

MOLERRO'S MENAGERIES

Park View Road
Ealing
London W5

June 1st, 2011

Ms Helen Costello
General Manager
The Hotel Endsleigh
Milton Abbot
Tavistock
Devon PL19 0PQ

Dear Ms Costello

Many thank yous for the letter of May 27th which was quite interesting regarding the pott-bellied pigg.

The Mrs does not eat cabling and pipework as far as we know although she does get through an extraordinary amount of cake.

Please could you send me the address of the children's farm where the pigg now lives.

Hoping to hear soon.

Yours sincerely

R Molerro (Mr)

Park View Road
Ealing
London W5

April 7th, 2011

The Secretary-General
The Kennel Club
1-5 Clarges Street
Piccadilly
London W1J 8AB

Dear Sir or Madam   **re: Dog Nuptials**

I wish to complain in the strongest possible terms to you, as the highest authority, about the ridiculous spectacle in this morning's papers, of two little dogs – Lola and Mugly - dressed up to the nines in wedding outfits and processing down the aisle together to specially selected wedding music, then off to a reception where 200 guests sat down to a spread including canapés, a duck and pheasant mousse, soup of the day, tasty titbits, and some scrag end of rump. The whole episode was absurd:

1 the so-called "bride" and "Groom" were, at 7 and 4 respectively, completely different ages, and wildly mismatched for any longstanding relationship. It's well known that the best age differential is to divide the groom's age by 2, add 8 and then (for cats and dogs) divide whatever's left by 7 (approx).

2 the clothing range was very poorly matched and ill fitting to boot. The bride (a yorkie by all accounts) sported Swarovski leg-cuffs which were clearly the wrong size and hung badly and accompanied by a silly ensemble of accoutrements including a bejewelled clutch bag. Mr Molierro noted that the groom was altogether more modestly attired with cast-offs picked up for next-to-nothing on eBay, which must have left him feeling very inferior. What sort of prospects there for mutual lifelong bliss? And the page boy Larry (described as "the bride's younger brother, aged 2") had a very tight and uncomfortable tux, topped off by a bowler hat of all things!

3 The colour scheme was inadequately thought through by the wedding planners and clashed with the bridesmaids (two pugs). The "happy couple" looked embarrassed and rather wan throughout this undignified occasion.

Can I ask candidly if the Kennel Club ordained this ceremony and were they represented at the nuptials?

Is there anything binding on the animals or are they free to roam elsewhere without commitment?

As a lifelong supporter of the KC I would be grateful for whatever assurances you can provide. One can only hope the couple are allowed some privacy for their honeymoon (in Catford presumably?) The whole thing has left me feeling quite ill.

 Yours sincerely,

Rosetta Molierro (Mrs)

Park View Road
Ealing
London W5

May 9th, 2011

Dame Fiona Reynolds
Head
The National Truss
PO Box 39
Warrington WA5 7WD

Dear Dame Reynolds

National Heritage site

I write at the instance of the wife (Mrs Molierro) who has some strong views on most things and is in no sense easy to shift. Nor is it at all advisable to try usually.

Mrs Molierro has recently undergone an intensive course of holistic mud and plaster therapy, with special attention to areas which I can't mention in this lettre (fundament etc).

Having diminished the pasta intake the Mrs now wishes to apply to be declared an Area of Outstanding Natural Beauty. Could you let me know if there's a form to fill in or something? She's already got a couple of cushions with AONB festooned on them, and a canopy over the chair similarly and a footstool.

Are there any acreage requirements involved? (we should be ok on this).

In my view a certificate recording the wife as a National Heritage site might be more appropriate, but this could be tricky as we had a bit of barney about it on the kitchen tableau last night and unfortunately there was a to-do what with some unusual words changing hands etc, and a minor incident with the cat being slightly kicked.

Hoping to hear soon in time for the Mrs' b'day in May as the wife's planning a party to celebrate the opening of the AONB award.

Looking forward to hearing. Apologies we're Italian.

Yours sincerely

R. Molierro (Mr)

PS: Beryl Trotfoot sends her best from that time she met you down at Bodiam Castle when she fell in the moat with her handbag and you helped haul her out with that winch thing when she nearly got beached.

2 June 2011

THE NATIONAL TRUST

HEELIS • KEMBLE DRIVE • SWINDON • WILTSHIRE SN2 2NA
Telephone +44 (0)1793 817664 • Facsimile +44 (0)1793 817401 • website www.nationaltrust.org.uk

Dear Mr Molière

Thank you for your letter of 9th
May to Fiona Reynolds.
We've had a chuckle in the
DG's office - your letter certainly

Dame Fiona Reynolds DBE
DIRECTOR-GENERAL

PTO →

Registered Charity Number 205846

gives a whole new meaning
to conservation!

thanks & best wishes
Michelle Merline
(Director-General's Coordinator)

END OF CORRESPONDENCE

191

If you have enjoyed this book,
do look out for more in the No.1 bestseller

The Morello Letters

Pen pal to the stars

Copies signed by the author, Mrs Morello and Enoch
the goat are available at www.morelloworld.com

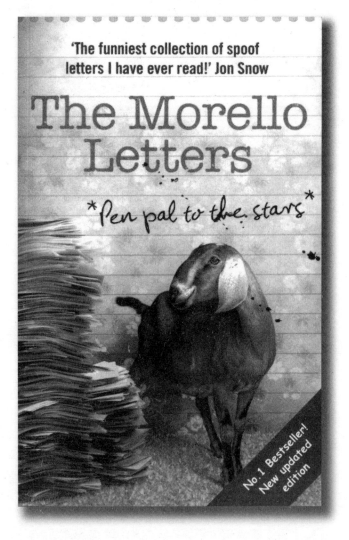